What Every Parent Needs to Know About 1st, 2nd & 3rd Grades

An Essential Guide to Your Child's Education

Toni S. Bickart
Diane Trister Dodge
Judy R. Jablon

Sourcebooks Inc.

Naperville, IL

Washington, DC

Co-published by:

Teaching Strategies, Inc.
P.O. Box 42243
Washington, DC 20015
(800) 637-3652
FAX: (202) 364-7273

Sourcebooks, Inc.
P.O. Box 372
Naperville, IL 60566
(630) 961-3900
FAX: (630) 961-2168

Internal illustrations by Jody Eastman
Author photo by Michael Bennett Kress

Library of Congress Cataloging-in-Publication Information
Bickart, Toni S.
What every parent needs to know about 1st, 2nd & 3rd grades: an essen-
tial guide to your child's education / Toni S. Bickart, Diane Trister Dodge,
Judy R. Jablon.
        p.   cm.
    Includes bibliographical references and index.
    ISBN 1-57071-156-9 (pbk. : alk. paper)
        1. Education, Primary—Parent participation—Handbooks, manu-
als, etc. I. Dodge, Diane Trister. II. Jablon, Judy R. III. Title.
    LB 1513.B45 1997
    372.24'1—dc21   97-1802
                                                          CIP

Printed and bound in the United States of America.
10 9 8 7 6 5 4 3 2 1

Table of Contents

Acknowledgments

Many people helped us to shape and refine this book. We are grateful to Joanna Phinney for moving us along as we began the task. We are indebted to Sybil Wolin for her thoughtful exploration of the message we wanted to convey, her guidance in helping us find the "voice," as well as her passionate editing. Without Larry Bram's conviction and creativity, we would not have this book. Emily Kohn asked the hard questions and made us defend our answers. Many people reviewed drafts and offered valuable suggestions. We would like to thank particularly Dr. Veneeta Acson, Selene Almazan of the Maryland Coalition for Inclusive Education, Richard and Michal Atkins, Debbie Billet-Roumell, Sue Bolin, Laura Bram, Cindy Easton, Suzanne M. Glazer, Gaye Gronlund, Jo Harriet Haley, Sheryl Kagen, Therese Keegan, Dr. Richard Lodish, Leigh Manasevit, Nikki Meyer, Leslie Rossen, Cynthia Scherr, Claudia Simmons, Betty Simon Thomas, Pattie Wilce, and Dianne Worthy.

Three of our colleagues shared their classroom expertise and experiences as staff developers which greatly enhanced the book—Pam Becker, Elizabeth Servidio, and Charlotte Stetson. We are indebted to the many teachers in schools all over the United States who allowed us into their classrooms and inspired us to tell their stories.

And finally, we want to acknowledge our partners at Sourcebooks. This is the first time Teaching Strategies has co-published a book and it has been a pleasure. We appreciate the efforts of Dominique Raccah, Karen Bouris, Renee Calomino, and Amanda Merrill. Special thanks to Todd Stocke, our editor, whose thoughtful questions helped to make this book better.

Foreword

American education purports to solve all kinds of problems—political, social, and economic—simultaneously. Unlike other nations, we rely on our educational institutions not only to educate children, but to instill democratic principles, realign practices of injustice, and keep us scientifically and economically competitive with other nations. Year after year, we play out our most poignant national dramas in our schools: we integrate schools before—and as a means to—integrating society; we offer parents due process to undo decades of injustice to citizens who are disabled. Within the context of education, immigration, and privatization, issues of importance to the American social fabric are also played out.

It is no wonder that Americans remain profoundly disappointed in their schools—despite the fact that children are achieving about as well as they did a quarter century ago according to the National Assessment for Educational Programs. And indeed, in some areas, there has been considerable progress. Between 1982 and 1992, for example, American students at ages 9, 13, and 17 (the intervals at which national data are collected) improved their overall performance in mathematics and science.

These accomplishments are especially noteworthy in light of the increased challenges facing American schools. We know, for example, that while poverty levels for the nation have not changed significantly in the last two decades, the rate of child poverty has escalated dramatically, so that today one in four U.S. children lives in poverty. We know that more children are growing up in households with declining economic prospects—more single-parent households and more households with a lower percentage of employed males.

Despite these challenges, America wants its schools to ready students for the demands of a new century—demands that are sure to command new skills and new approaches to problem-solving. Today's students need not only the basic competencies of education in the past, but also a broad understanding of their world and its diverse peoples and cultures; they need to develop their analytic and interpretive skills so they can respond to this new world and the information it generates; they need the intellectual curiosity and agility to challenge new frontiers; they need the communicative and interpersonal skills to hurdle the demands of life in a society more complex and pressured than ever before. We are now being called on to create the 21st Century student: the independent, analytic problem-solver; the inventive, break-the-mold thinker; the effective collaborator; and the reflective, competent citizen.

Can schools do all this? Can they really meet all the challenges they face? Can they simultaneously be bastions of educational excellence and hubs of comprehensive, integrated services? Can they serve the nation's socio-political agenda while preparing children for their lives in a volatile intellectual and technological world? The answer is no, they cannot—and yet they must, because no other institution is more pivotal to the future of the society than our schools. And that is where this book comes in.

Whether as volunteers in the PTA, PTO, or Head Start Policy Councils, parents have been central to the mission of schooling.

And with good reason. Parental involvement produces results. We know, for example, that when parents are involved, their children's achievement improves. We also know that parent education and parent involvement programs produce better student attendance, fewer referrals to special education, higher graduation rates, and greater enrollment in post-secondary education.

Always necessary, the push for parent involvement has never been more pronounced—or more complicated. School rules and policies change abruptly. Yesterday's fads are today's teaching trends. Policies enacted only weeks ago quickly become outdated and are overtaken by new ones. Yesterday's curriculum has been replaced by today's kit or packaged learning materials. Parents find themselves amidst a sea of reform where flux is never-ending. To educators, this flux is so prevalent that it is accepted as normal. For parents, however, these constant changes are mysterious and complicated. Rather than having a clear picture of their roles, rights, and responsibilities, parents are plunged into an ever-changing sea of new ideas and trends.

Parents need help and schools need help. *What Every Parent Needs to Know about 1st, 2nd & 3rd Grades* does both. It makes the strange seem routine; the unpredictable seem predictable; the foreign seem knowable; the questionable seem comprehensible. It is a treasure of facts and frameworks, guiding families and schools into better, more positive linkages with one another.

Reading this book is a delight. It is well-organized and chock full of precisely the information parents want to and should know. Taking a balanced perspective on education, it provides concrete strategies and questions for parents. It's a magical tool kit—with instructions—for learning all that's important to know about the classroom. The checklists, graphics, and clear, direct questions should be excellent guides for parents, which will enrich both their experience and their children's school experience.

At a time when more is being demanded of children, parents, and schools, this is an invaluable resource, poised to help them all achieve these ends.

–SHARON L. KAGAN, ED.D.

Senior Associate, The Bush
Center in Child Development
and Social Policy, Yale University

April, 1997

Preface

When children reach first grade, schools typically have a new set of expectations. Some of these expectations are reasonable; others may not be. In this book we highlight what children are like in first, second, and third grades—the primary grades—and explain why some of these expectations are appropriate and why others are not.

Six year olds generally show a big leap in development. They are beginning to reason and think logically, with an increased ability to understand cause and effect and to organize information in systematic ways. These new cognitive abilities enable them to take on new tasks and learning opportunities. However, six year olds still need many experiences that help them develop socially, emotionally, and physically. In the primary grades, particularly, it is necessary to ensure a good balance.

When school works for children, they begin to believe that they are competent and that school is a good place for them. We wrote this book for parents who want to know how first, second, and third grade classrooms can be exciting and interesting places for children to learn. Our goal is to offer an in-depth look at children of this age and how they learn best.

For too many parents, information about schools and classroom practices has been limited to what is reported by the media. Typically, information in the news highlights major controversies with a focus on extreme positions, and gives parents little guidance on how to figure out what is going on in their own child's classroom. Parents interpret what they see based on the impressions they developed as students themselves and a vision of school that is both incomplete and perhaps twenty-five to thirty-five years out of date. You wouldn't want a doctor to treat you using only information known and practiced a quarter of a century ago. Similarly, our children deserve an education based on the accumulated research of many years and on the best practices of teachers and schools across the country.

This book is based on the work we do as staff developers with classroom teachers as well as our own experiences as teachers. Several years ago we wrote a book for teachers called *Constructing Curriculum for the Primary Grades*. We stressed the importance of communicating with and involving parents in their child's education. Realizing how little information about learning in the classroom is available for parents, we decided to write a book that would meet that need.

As teacher trainers and educators, we work with schools all across the country helping teachers think about how to teach. We know that the ideas in this book are real and practical—we've seen them in action. The stories of teachers and children are our stories and those of teachers we have coached and from whom we have learned.

We hope to help you to see what is involved in learning to read and write, so you know what to ask about and look for in your child's classroom. How do you know if your child's math lessons are appropriately challenging? And, what about science and social studies? What does it mean for a six, seven, or eight year old to do research and conduct experiments? Which is better—studying lots of subjects or a few in depth? Is more homework better or does it depend on what kind it is? What kind of information do you get about how your child is doing? Does it tell you what you need to know? We answer these questions, give you ideas for activities to do at home with your child, and suggest questions to ask your child's teacher. There is also a list of recommended resources in the back of the book in case you want to know more about the content of the curriculum, child development, school reform, learning disabilities, special needs, inclusion, national standards, and World Wide Web sites of interest to parents.

With this book, we take you inside real classrooms to see how children can learn in an environment that promotes intellectual growth and social competence, where children learn skills and knowledge and respect and responsibility. Classrooms such as these don't just happen; teachers purposefully create these classrooms each year with every new group of children they teach.

We hope this book will offer you:

- a new way to look at your child's classroom
- help in choosing a school for your child
- a vocabulary to describe and reflect on what you see
- a knowledge of how children learn
- information about best practices
- questions to ask of teachers, administrators, other parents, and your child
- ways to develop a partnership with your child's teacher

Our message is that classrooms can be exciting places where meaningful and substantive learning occurs. You can find out if this is happening in your child's classroom. We hope our book will help you to begin.

–Toni S. Bickart
Diane Trister Dodge
Judy R. Jablon
Washington, DC
April, 1997

– 1 –
Learning in the Early Grades

Entering elementary school is a big step for your child; it is also a big step for you. The early elementary grades are a crucial stage in your child's life when important academic skills should be learned. Undoubtedly, there are times when you may feel confused, anxious, or in the dark because you don't understand what's happening in your child's classroom or why.

Several years ago we wrote *Constructing Curriculum for the Primary Grades.*[1] Our goal in that book was to give teachers strategies for making curriculum meaningful and effective for children. Now we are writing to address the issues that concern parents.

Questions Parents Ask

"Why is my child learning a letter a week when he already knows how to read?"

"My child thinks he's reading, but he guesses at so many words. Why won't they teach him to sound out words?"

"Why can't I figure out what the curriculum is and what my child is supposed to be learning?"

"Is my child really learning math if I never see any worksheets?"

"Why isn't my child learning the rules for doing addition and subtraction? What's all this nonsense about trying to solve problems different ways?"

"Why are the children working all over the place—at tables, on the floor? Why can't they sit at desks for their work?"

"Why does my child come home with work that has misspelled words? Why haven't they been corrected?"

"My child is always being asked to help other children with reading and writing. Isn't this a waste of time for her? Isn't the teacher supposed to be doing the teaching?"

"I don't understand my child's new report card. Where are the letter grades?"

"My child is miserable in 1st grade. He was so happy in Kindergarten. What's wrong?"

"My child writes all the time but I don't think she's really learning to spell and punctuate. When will these skills be taught?"

"There is all this work in groups. What about my child's individual talents?"

"My child can't do the homework on her own. How much time should I spend helping her?"

"All the lessons are geared to one level. My child needs more challenging work in math and extra help in spelling. How are his needs going to be met?"

Parents need and deserve to have their questions answered. So much confusing information is being bandied about and issues are becoming unnecessarily polarized. As teachers of young children, as staff developers working with teachers and schools, and as parents, we have struggled with these issues.

We believe that schools must help all children acquire important skills and knowledge. We value a rigorous curriculum that responds to the individual and developmental needs of children. And we know that successful educational practices for first, second, and third graders must be designed with the six-to-eight year old child in mind.

What Six-to-Eight Year Olds Are Like

"I'm beginning to wonder who my child has become. One minute he's friendly and enthusiastic and the next, he's arguing with me about everything or whining like a baby."

"I can't keep up with who her best friend is because it changes daily."

"He's so critical of himself. He erases with such intensity, he makes holes in the paper."

"She can really be interesting to be around. You can have a real conversation and talk about opinions."

These observations by parents have captured many of the contradictions and growing pains of six-to-eight year olds who are trying to figure out who they are and how they appear to others. The psychologist Erik Erikson described children between six and eight as being in the "Stage of Industry."[2] They like to create projects and want to do a job well. If they have opportunities to apply the skills they are developing, they feel competent. By competent we mean sure enough of themselves to take risks and to struggle with challenges in order to reach a goal, solve a problem, or complete a task. Children who don't have a sense of their own competence tend to feel inferior. "I can't do it" becomes their refrain. Erikson's theories explain how important appropriate challenges are in order for children to feel successful. The classroom practices that we describe in the course of this book are designed to promote exploration and make striving toward a goal intrinsically satisfying.

Stanley Greenspan, a noted child psychiatrist, describes these years as the time when children move beyond viewing themselves as the center of the universe and enter the "rough-and-tumble world of peer relationships."[3] They define who they are and how they view themselves in relation to others—primarily their peer group. Greenspan's theories demonstrate how important it is for children to have time to practice the skills of both working with others and being independent. As educators and parents, we want children to develop socially and emotionally in order for them to become teenagers and adults who can face challenges and make decisions for a healthy and successful life.

Principles That Make Learning Effective

Our extensive work as staff developers has taken us to schools all over the country. We have worked with both new teachers and experienced teachers in inner city schools, in small rural schools, in suburban schools, and in both public and private schools. We have collaborated with principals and teachers who are working to make changes in their programs so that instruction is more effective. It is clear that great classrooms have much in common. They aren't exactly the same, but they share a set of underlying educational principles.

Following are the principles that we have seen in operation in excellent classrooms around the country:

Learning is active. Children are doers—they are ready to explore the world around them to learn how things work. Active learning capitalizes on this eagerness to learn. By handling materials, interviewing people, and taking trips, for example, children's understanding deepens and their learning solidifies. Hands-on experiences enable children to move from the concrete to more abstract levels of learning.

Learning is challenging. Challenging work is difficult enough to stretch children, but it is also within their reach. Work that is too easy for children fails to motivate them. Work that is too hard defeats them. When work is carefully balanced to challenge children, they feel competent and proud when they complete it. Challenging work requires time to study and explore issues in depth and should be accompanied by encouraging messages from teachers and parents, "You can do it. I will help you to succeed."

Learning is varied. Assignments and lessons should not all look alike or require the same kind of product. When children are introduced to new concepts and are given chances to represent them—by making charts or graphs, drawing pictures, creating computer designs or diagrams, building models, putting on skits, or describing it in their own words, they increase their understanding and learn to use different skills to communicate.[4] Different modes of representation also challenge children to think about their learning in new ways.[5] And finally, children have different learning styles—what works for some children may not work for others.

Learning is meaningful. Meaningful learning is engaging because children see a connection to the real world. In great classrooms, the projects assigned, topics studied, and the lessons taught are both interesting and relevant to children. According to several studies, when children understand the relevance of what they are learning, they are more likely to approach these activities with a positive attitude.[6] Moreover, children tend to retain what they have learned when they have a reason and desire to discover something. Current research about how children learn and how the brain functions confirms that human beings remember more when they know why they are learning something and when they can connect it to what they already know.[7]

Learning is collaborative. Collaborative learning takes place formally when children work with one or more classmates on a project or task with specific goals in mind. It takes place informally throughout the day when children working at tables turn to their peers for help or to share ideas. As they collaborate they acquire social skills—taking turns, sharing, giving and getting help, listening to others. They also work on their academic skills—designing questions, discussing and trying out ideas, explaining their findings to others. In the process of interacting, children clarify their own thinking and can master new subject matter.

Learning is a shared responsibility. Sharing responsibility means that the family, the teacher, and the child all contribute to the learning process. Parents, who have been teaching the child since birth, share valuable information with teachers. The teacher provides a clear structure and serves as a guide, knowing when to challenge children to investigate on their own and when to teach specific skills that will assist them in their explorations. Children know what the expectations are, develop a plan, and carry out their work with more and more independence. As a result of sharing, children take charge of their own behavior. Values are learned—values that are basic to a democratic society. These values include self-respect, respect for others, and a sense of responsibility for the community and the environment.

Why Schools Need to Be Different Today

There is lots of talk about the failure of our schools and what has to be done to give children a world-class education. But, there is confusion about how this translates into day to day practice. Understandably, parents have many doubts.

"But, school wasn't like this for me and I turned out okay. We sat at desks, filled in workbook pages, and followed the rules. Sure, a lot of it was boring, but we learned. Why should it be different today?"

Teachers have their concerns as well.

"I wasn't taught to teach this way. I'm used to standing in front of the room, teaching a concept, and then giving children materials to practice what I have taught. Why should I change?"

The educational practices of previous generations were designed to prepare students for a workplace with very different demands from the workplace of the 21st Century. Analyses of our changing economy indicate that the workplace our children will enter requires both additional and higher level skills. With fewer manufacturing jobs available, children are entering a workforce where they will work as part of a team. To function in the "information" age, children must not only know how to access knowledge but also how to apply information effectively. They must be able to solve problems and work with others.

Moreover, parents and children are under enormous pressure. Parents are working harder, they are experiencing more stress, and there is frequently little support from extended families, who are geographically distant. Whereas in the past children came home from school and played with friends, many children today are not allowed to play outside because of safety concerns. Others are enrolled in special after school activities to keep them safe and busy until parents come home from work. Children are exposed from an early age to cultural influences that glorify violence and drugs. Many watch endless hours of TV. They have fewer opportunities to play informally with friends, talk with adults, or read for pleasure. The skills, attitudes, and understandings they need to become productive citizens and succeed in the job market of the 21st Century have to be learned.

Extensive research about the brain during the last ten years has also had an impact on our understandings about how children learn. First, we now know that environment and experience can have a tremendous influence on the development of intelligence.[8] Second, new studies of intelligence have confirmed that there are many ways to be intelligent.[9] Rather than looking at each child and asking, "How smart is this child?" we should rephrase the question and ask "How is *this* child smart?" thereby acknowledging that each child has unique strengths. Third, a child's ability to use their unique strengths positively may depend on their emotional intelligence—whether they know how to "read" feelings and whether they can control their impulses and delay gratification.[10]

Schools cannot continue to rely on practices from the past. It is irresponsible to ignore research about how the brain works, about the role of emotional intelligence in children's ability to succeed, about skill development in language and literacy, and about how mathematical and scientific thinking are nurtured in the classroom. Our children deserve an education that reflects the most up-to-date thinking and educators who consider not only what they teach, but how they teach.

What to Look For

> *"OK, so even if I agree that things are different today, really, how can I possibly evaluate what's happening in my child's classroom? What should I do? Walk in and ask the teacher a lot of questions? She'll resent me and my child will be worse off."*

You have a right to know what is happening in your child's classroom. You have the right to go and look. Many of the characteristics of great classrooms we describe in this book can be observed in a first visit where you just look around the room at what is on the walls and how furniture and materials are arranged. Subsequent visits and the work your child talks about or brings home will tell you more. Parent/teacher conferences will give you additional information. Get the feel of what is going on.

We suggest you use the principles of learning we described on pages 5-7 as a guide to assess what you see in your child's classroom, the work your child brings home, and what you learn when you talk with your child and the teacher about school work. Use these principles as the basis for creating a checklist to guide your observations. On the next page is an example of how a checklist might look. Reading the chapters that follow will help you to complete your own. Don't expect to be able to fill it in immediately. Over the course of many months and many observations you will be able to consider what and how your child should be learning in first, second, and third grade.

A Parent's Checklist

PRINCIPLES	OBSERVATIONS
Learning is active	Saw lots of math materials in the classroom. Kids used them during a math work time. J worked in the science area using a magnifying glass to study a mealworm.
Learning is challenging	J is so excited about his project on insects that I couldn't get him to go to bed on time. This is the first time he's asked to go to the library to get books.
Learning is varied	Lots of children's art work on display. The pictures are all different from one another. J got to organize a puppet show on the book his group just finished. Very excited!
Learning is meaningful	J says he is doing a project about how we get food. Asking lots of questions about where I buy food. Wants to go to the supermarket, interested in how they get deliveries.
Learning is collaborative	Writing a story with his friend Sean. Kids worked in groups to plan interviews of people who work in the supermarket. Different size tables in classroom. Kids seem to regroup a lot.
Learning is a shared responsibility	Lots of materials for children to use — everything is super organized and kids clean up! J was working in a small group when I came in. Seemed to know what they had to do. Teacher was in another part of room with another group.

Your Checklist

PRINCIPLES	OBSERVATIONS
Learning is active	
Learning is challenging	
Learning is varied	
Learning is meaningful	
Learning is collaborative	
Learning is a shared responsibility	

How to Get Involved

Research clearly demonstrates that when parents are involved in their child's school life everyone benefits.[11] Parents who develop a partnership with their children's teachers feel accepted in the school community and more confident about helping their child. Teachers also gain from a partnership. They gain needed support and respect from parents and find that children are more cooperative. And most importantly, children show evidence of increased achievement.

There are different ways for parents to learn about what is happening in their child's school and to get involved. One way is to visit the classroom and observe first hand what the environment is like and how children work. Remember that teachers and children need time to get into the rhythm of the year. So it is wise to wait a few weeks until the school year is well underway before you visit. Don't walk in unannounced. Call first and tell the teacher you would like to observe. Ask when a good time would be and if there is anything he or she would like you to help with while you visit. Try to observe a lesson or work time and think about the principles we describe. Take the checklist with you and look at what children are doing and what the teacher is doing.

Talk with your child about life in his or her classroom. Try to avoid asking "What did you learn in school today?" To this question, our children most often answered, "Nothing." Instead, use the principles on the checklist to help you think about other questions you might ask.

- "Did you get to use any special materials in your work today?" *(learning is active)*

- "What are you working on in math these days?" *(learning is challenging)*

- "Did you get to do any projects today with a friend?" *(learning is collaborative)*

Look at the homework assignments and the completed projects your child brings home. Consider them in light of the principles and the information in subsequent chapters.

You don't have to wait for the first parent-teacher conference to talk with your child's teacher. As soon as school starts, begin keeping a list of your questions and concerns, as well as a note about something that is going well. After a few weeks have passed, call the teacher and make an appointment. Talk about something positive first and say you want to talk about your child—his or her interests, strengths, learning style, and any special needs. Ask the teacher for any insights about how your child relates to others, approaches new tasks, and seeks help. Don't challenge—ask questions about why a teacher does things. Explain that you want to be supportive and ask how you can help. Share with the teacher what you observed and any concerns you have.

The next chapter describes the classroom conditions that promote effective learning. In the following chapters we discuss how children learn to read and write, do math, and explore topics in social studies and science. Our examples show how the principles we mentioned earlier are put into action. You'll see the many ways children learn and how different kinds of opportunities—art, music, drama, movement, technology—support learning. At the end of each chapter you will find suggestions of activities to do at home with your child to support the kind of learning practices we describe. They are designed to help children make the connection between what they are learning in school and the real world. We also provide questions for you to use when you have a parent/teacher conference. They will help you find out more about the classroom practices in your child's classroom.

All of our children deserve great classrooms. Parents have a very important role to play in making their child's school the best it can be.

– 2 –
The Best Classroom
for Your Child

A child who looks forward to going to school is a lot easier to live with and is more likely to succeed as a learner than a child who is unhappy at school. In this book we describe children who are happy in classrooms where they feel competent and successful academically and socially. We show how children can learn to read, write, think mathematically and scientifically, and explore social studies in ways that are interesting and challenging. Before turning to the specifics of how children learn these subjects, we will discuss the conditions that prevail in classrooms where children are happy and eager to learn.

Just as a plant needs fertile ground and sunlight to grow to its full potential, children learn best in classrooms where the conditions are right. What are these conditions? We believe that the classroom should function as a workplace with a clear structure that everyone understands. We also believe that the classroom should function as a community where children see themselves as joined together for a common purpose–to learn.

The Classroom as a Workplace

Think about the different places you have worked. Each has its own structure. Do people work behind closed doors with little interaction? Are decisions made through formal channels? Maybe the best ideas get discussed around the water fountain or over a cup of coffee. When people talk about structure in the classroom, they frequently have different views in mind. One kind of structure is totally teacher directed or authoritarian. The teacher dictates all the rules. He or she is the only source of information about what to do and when to do it. Children, in effect, obey orders. While this approach may make for a quiet, orderly classroom (as long as the teacher is present), it is not likely to help your child develop self-discipline and take responsibility for his or her own learning.

There can also be structure in a classroom where the teacher has authority but is not authoritarian. In this setting the teacher works with children to establish a sense of order based not on power, but on the mutual agreement that everyone is there to learn. This is what you might experience upon entering such a classroom.

> *You hear a steady hum of activity. At first you don't see the teacher; she is sitting with one of several small groups of children working on math activities at tables arranged in different areas of the room. Each group of children is using a set of materials together. They are talking about what they are doing, explaining their ideas, giving directions, asking questions, and laughing. You sit down with one group and ask what they are doing. One child volunteers: "We are finding out how many ways we can make different shapes. See, we've made triangles, squares, and diamonds," he says. You then ask, "How did you know what to do?" Another child explains, "We had a meeting and talked about different shapes we knew. Then each group got different things to use. We got the geoboards, that group got popsicle sticks, over there they have tangrams." Just before you leave, the teacher calls the children together in the meeting area so each group can report on what they did.*

This teacher has worked to create a climate where responsibility is shared, responding to the need of children this age to have autonomy and feel competent. Because the teacher doesn't hold all the cards, children can act independently. Even when the teacher is not present with a group, the children know what is expected and act accordingly.

You may be concerned that a structure based on mutual understanding means that anything goes. We, too, would be concerned about a classroom with a laissez-faire structure. We advocate establishing a structure that is clear and predictable. The best structure should be obvious by evaluating the:

- physical arrangement of the classroom

- placement and accessibility of materials and supplies

- daily schedule and routines

- rules

The Physical Arrangement of the Classroom

How furniture is arranged can tell you a great deal about the structure in a classroom. Some arrangements are more likely to support the learning principles on your checklist than others. For example, when desks are arranged in rows facing the teacher's desk in front, children receive the message that they are expected to keep their eyes on the teacher and passively listen and follow directions. Rather than promoting shared responsibility, the very placement of the furniture encourages dependency. Such an arrangement does not encourage active learning either. Nor does it enable children to work collaboratively easily. A different message is sent when the classroom has a special area for children to meet to talk as a whole group, and when the furniture is arranged for children to work in a variety of ways, in pairs, in small groups, and alone. This message is: "In this classroom, we help each other to learn."

Just as you learn to work in different work environments, children have to be taught how to work productively in a classroom. For example, learning how to participate in discussions, when to get materials, where to find them, and where to take them to begin work are some skills children learn. When the classroom environment is used well, you are more likely to see some or all of the principles in operation. What if your child's classroom doesn't resemble our description? Effective learning may still be taking place. But, because it may be more difficult to see the principles in action, you will have to look harder to see how or if children are learning effectively.

Placement and Accessibility of Materials and Supplies

The arrangement of materials and supplies also tells you about the structure of the classroom. In a classroom where the teacher recognizes learning as a shared responsibility, materials are available for children to use and put away as needed. In that way, children do not have to wait for the teacher to distribute materials. What's more, the very act of selecting materials and putting them away is a part of the learning process. Learning about order and responsibility occurs daily. In addition, when children have to choose what tools they need for a particular project, they function as active learners, solving problems and making logical decisions.

The classrooms of effective teachers may look different from one another, but there is a logical order to the display and selection of materials.

- A particular place for each set of materials in storage units or library folders

- Low shelves so materials are accessible

- Labels on containers and shelves so that things can easily be put away in their proper places

- Shared materials—such as pencils, crayons, and scissors— in containers so children can take them to the tables

When materials and supplies are arranged this way, children can be involved in matters of routine classroom care to further promote shared responsibility. Later, in Chapter 6, *How Children Learn Social Studies*, we will discuss a process for developing a job chart and responsibilities for clean-up.

The Daily Schedule and Routines

The daily schedule shows blocks of time and how the time will be spent. Routines are the procedures for how children do activities and move from one activity to another. Children who know what to expect each day are helped to feel in control and secure. They can stay on task or move from one activity to the next because they know the routine. Look for a daily schedule posted in your child's classroom.

Note whether there seems to be a balance of active and quiet activities, times when children can work on projects together, times for instruction in various subjects, and times for children to be outdoors.

Each classroom has its own way of doing things. Many teachers have special routines to start or end the day and they vary from year to year depending on the group of children. Your child may talk about class songs, a special activity every Friday afternoon, specific routines for cleaning up, lining up, going to the bathroom, and so on. Routines help to provide structure because once children learn them, they can function independently and with confidence.

Rules

Teachers who recognize that shared responsibility is an important learning principle involve children in the process of making rules for classroom life. We have observed that when children are not involved in rule making, there tend to be more management problems in the classroom with children acting out or otherwise challenging the teacher. In our experience, children are more likely to obey rules that they helped to create. Many teachers we have worked with begin the year by saying something like this to children: "How can we make our classroom a safe, comfortable, and happy place for everyone?" As children suggest ideas, they write them on a chart. From this discussion rules for the classroom evolve, for example:

- Be helpful to others.

- Solve problems with words.

- Keep the room neat and organized.

- Move slowly in the classroom.

- Treat others the way you want them to treat you.

Many classrooms have posted rules. The distinguishing characteristic in a classroom that promotes shared responsibility is that children helped to generate the rules and children take responsibility for making sure they are followed. Generating the rules is only the first step. Children need many reminders, and the opportunity to re-evaluate the rules they develop. Everyone shares responsibility for living by the rules; it's not just up to the teacher.

If behavior and defiance of rules seem to be an issue for your child, rulemaking might be something you want to investigate further. Begin by talking to your child about whether there are classroom rules and how they came to be. Then talk to your child's teacher about how you can work together to help your child become invested in following the rules.

The Classroom as a Community

Every classroom, like every community, has its own distinct values, goals, and activities. When teachers create a community in the classroom, children feel connected to one another. A group spirit emerges that says "We're all in this together." Classrooms that function as communities are responsive to the need of six-to-eight year olds to "belong" while enabling teachers to implement the important principles for learning.

We have found that in successful classroom communities children typically:

- are helped to make friends
- learn respect for others
- resolve conflicts peacefully
- learn together

Making Friends

Peer relationships are a central social issue for children six-to-eight years old. Having friends can make the difference between a happy child and one who is lonely and ill at ease around others. Yet, despite the importance of friendships, many primary grade children are not skilled in making and keeping friends.

You probably have some idea whether your child makes friends easily or has a hard time establishing friendships. Children who do not have friends or who are repeatedly rejected by their peers are in a cycle of rejection that they often cannot break out of on their own. To break this cycle, children need the help of a caring adult. Teachers who recognize the importance of friendships consciously teach skills children need to make friends and plan ways to promote friendships among the children in the classroom.

In a classroom conducive to friend-making skills, children can have discussions about behaviors that are likely to be accepted–smiling, asking questions, offering ideas, inviting someone to play, or offering to share something. Many excellent children's books can be used to introduce the subject of friendship and to stimulate a discussion. After reading and discussing stories children can, for example, work in small groups to make up skits based on the plot and perform them for the class. When teachers create opportunities for pairs or small groups to work together, children get to work with peers they wouldn't normally choose. Children can be paired to do jobs, play games, work on art, read, and do math. Building friendships in the classroom builds a sense of community.

Respecting Others

Not everyone in the class is likely to be your child's friend. Children need to learn, however, that they can get along with people, even people they don't particularly like. In a successful classroom community, children learn to respect others and get along with everyone.

Children learn from what they see. Caring, empathetic teachers set a powerful example. When children are treated with respect, they are more likely to treat others the same way. The more we work with teachers the more we believe that the most effective teachers devote time and energy to modeling respectful interactions. They do this daily in the way they greet children in the morning and say good-bye at the end of the day. When children are greeted by name, when a personal connection is made about something that happened the day before, for example, they begin the day feeling good and can make positive connections with others. Children will use words such as "please" and "thank you" and "I'm sorry for interrupting," when teachers remember to use these terms regularly in the classroom.

Sometimes modeling is not sufficient; teachers have to be more active about teaching children how to interact in respectful ways. A teacher using more active methods of building respect might do role playing activities to help children develop social skills and read books to generate discussions on the topic of being respectful.

Resolving Conflicts

If children can't control their emotions, they are at risk for academic failure and other serious problems.[12] Children can learn to handle intense emotions, including anger, without resorting to aggression. Resolving conflicts peacefully requires that all those involved feel their views have been heard and feel they have contributed to a solution. Many primary grade children are just learning to put their feelings into words—a prerequisite for learning to handle conflicts. Even those with well-developed language skills may lose their ability to express themselves in the heat of anger or hurt feelings.

While six-to-eight year olds are cognitively capable of seeing a situation from another person's point of view, this ability is often lost in the midst of a conflict. The conflicts that typically arise in first, second, and third grade classrooms are likely to include: whose turn it is to be first at something, getting in each other's "space," who is friends with whom, who took someone's belongings, who got something first. Your child is more likely to learn skills in conflict resolution if the teacher incorporates conflict resolution strategies into the curriculum.

We have observed effective teachers helping children to resolve conflicts in the following ways:

- *Modeling how to handle anger.* Teachers talk about how they feel. They say they are upset about how the class behaved in the lunchroom, for example, and that they will talk about the incident after collecting their thoughts. They talk about strategies they use when they feel themselves getting angry—for example, stopping and counting to 10, taking five deep breaths.

- *Using class meetings to discuss how to handle conflicts.* Discussions can take place when the atmosphere is calm to consider something upsetting that happened at another time during the day—at recess, in the lunchroom, during clean up time. Role plays, where children act out what happened or a situation from a book are also a vehicle for teaching conflict resolution skills.

- *Developing a list of steps children can use to solve problems.* First the parties to the problem have to calm down. The subsequent steps usually include: identifying the problem, generating solutions, agreeing on a solution and trying it, evaluating the solution, and sharing the results.

- *Designating a "calm down" area in the classroom.* Because group life is demanding, many teachers establish one or two places in the classroom where children can go to cool off, relax, or take a break as a positive alternative to acting out or falling apart during a conflict.

To support what teachers do in the classroom, many schools have adopted particular conflict resolution programs that are taught school wide to children, teachers, and parent volunteers. Each program has its own language for what to say and do and a step-by-step process to follow when there is a conflict. If this subject is a concern of yours, you may want to find out whether your child's school is involved in such a program.

Learning Together

The kind of community that supports successful learning requires that children realize they are working together toward common goals. Children don't necessarily enter first grade knowing how to work well with others. They need to learn these skills by working with partners and in small groups. With practice and coaching, children learn to take turns, share, give help to others, and accept help from peers. The classroom community builds the message that, "in this classroom, we help one another learn."

Our observations that children benefit from working together are confirmed by research. Children's relationships with peers, especially those of different ethnic, socio-economic, and ability groups, are improved through learning together.[13]

We have found that meetings—group discussions—which involve the whole class are one of the most effective ways to build a learning community in the classroom. Throughout the day, whenever the group as a whole needs to talk together, a designated meeting area is used as a gathering place. In this environment children learn how to listen to others, and how to talk so that others can understand. Meetings serve many purposes. In meetings, for example, children:

- greet one another and review plans for the day
- discuss what the class is learning
- talk about and generate solutions to a problem that occurs at recess
- listen to and discuss a story
- learn about the proper use and care of classroom materials
- discuss the activities for a work time
- talk about the next activity
- hear a report

By participating in meetings, your child will learn what it means to be part of a community in which all members share ideas and listen to one another.

As you observe in your child's classroom, talk with your child about school, look at the work he or she brings home, and conference with your child's teacher, consider the nature of the classroom environment—how it functions as a workplace and as a successful learning community.

How Parents Can Help

- Discuss and agree on ways to store games, books, and clothing so that your child can find things independently and put them away at home.

- Talk about the jobs that need to be done in the family and agree on how they will be handled.

- Make schedules together of when to do homework and when to play.

- Help your child invite friends from school to your home to play, for example, by initiating the phone call, if necessary.

- Talk about the rules that are important for your family to function, for example, about mealtimes or laundry responsibilities. Develop them together.

- When conflicts arise at home, ask your child to help think of solutions.

Questions to Ask Your Child's Teacher

- How do you help children develop a sense of responsibility and self-discipline?

- May I see an example of a daily schedule?

- Who are my child's friends?

- Is my child comfortable working with children other than his good friends?

- What opportunities are there during the day for children to work together?

- I know that my child sometimes has some trouble solving problems with friends. How do you help children work on conflict resolution skills?

- Do you involve children in group discussions about social issues and about what they are learning?

- Are there some materials you would like to have in the classroom that I can contribute?

– 3 –
How Children
Become Readers

"Guess what! We just finished reading The Shoeshine Girl *(by Clyde Robert Bulla). I loved it. My group is doing a skit about the book. I need shoe polish and a brush for the skit. Do we have that? Can I take them to school?"*

Children need experiences to connect them personally with books. From these experiences, they discover that reading is an enjoyable and interesting part of classroom life. Reading has many purposes— to get information, to explore ideas, to learn about people, to visit far away places. Teaching reading involves helping children learn strategies so they can understand the meaning of what they read. At the same time reading instruction should highlight the pleasures and benefits of being a reader.

Children begin "reading" long before they enter elementary school. As infants and toddlers, they enjoy looking through books with adults. Eventually they learn to connect the pictures in a book with the words on the page. You may remember how your child asked you to read the same books over and over again. Children enjoy repetition—they love to anticipate what happens next and delight in knowing the answer. Once they have discovered that the words on the page say the same thing every time, children will correct an adult who omits or substitutes a word in a familiar book. They will pretend to read a well-loved book on their own. They may retell the story, pause as they turn the pages, and even change their tone of voice for different characters. These actions are key reading behaviors.

Viewing themselves as readers, children are motivated to develop the skills they need. Reading experiences in school should use this natural enthusiasm to propel your child to become a lifelong reader.

What's Involved in Learning to Read

Children need to learn that reading is getting meaning from print.
Readers know that written words convey messages. Children develop
strategies to help them get the big ideas or the gist of a story. For
example, they might:

- Look for pictures that explain the story.

- Ask themselves, "What's going to happen next?"

- Skip the hard word and finish the sentence, then guess
  what word might fit the blank.

- Finish reading and try to remember what happened first,
  second, next…and last.

- Ask themselves, "Did what I read make sense?"

- Ask themselves, "What's this story about?"

***Children need many kinds of experiences to make sense of what
they read.*** Because reading involves making connections between
words and ideas, children need opportunities to hear new vocabulary,
talk about the meaning of words, and connect words with images.
With many varied experiences, children gain language skills and are
better able to connect new information to what they already know.
For example, a child who has seen and talked about bridges can
understand what the word *bridge* means when he or she reads it in a
book; a child who has seen an elephant at the zoo can look at the
word *elephant* in a book and make meaning from the individual
letters and sounds.

For children to become efficient readers, they have to understand about how reading works. For example, there are clues on each page. Reading proceeds from left to right and from the top of the page to the bottom. Each letter (or group of letters) is a symbol for a different sound and words are put together as combinations of letters. The words on paper are just like spoken words. Groups of words form sentences and paragraphs that have meaning.

To be good readers, children need many strategies to figure out what a word says. Children learn to read in different ways. For example, some children can see a word, immediately recognize it, and say it out loud. Others sound out the letters in words, and still others may guess a word based on a picture clue. Your child needs to learn several ways to decipher or decode words to make sense out of his or her reading. Decoding strategies should include the following:

- looking for pictures that help explain the story
- recognizing a word they have seen elsewhere
- thinking about what word sounds correct in the sentence
- recognizing the sounds made by letters or groups of letters

Children learn to read at different rates. Some children learn to read in preschool and kindergarten. Others may not read fluently until well into second or third grade. When children learn to read is not as important in the long term as how they feel about reading. Enjoyment and interest in reading inspire children to learn the skills needed to be good readers.

Phonics and Whole Language

You may have heard or read about the debate over the benefits of phonics versus whole language as the method for learning to read.

This debate has even entered the political arena at local, state, and national levels. We believe that often, the discussion is oversimplified and unnecessarily polarized.

Defining the Terms

Phonics is *one* of the strategies readers use to figure out unfamiliar words. When parents and teachers encourage children to "sound out" a word, they are asking them to think about the sounds attached to individual letters or groups of letters, and to use that information to "read" the word. In order to use phonics as a reading strategy, children must know about the sounds letters make. When most people talk about learning phonics, they envision drills in letter sounds and worksheets to match pictures and words.

When educators speak of *whole language* they are referring to a set of beliefs about how children acquire language skills. Drawing on a knowledge of child development, advocates of a whole language approach believe that children learn to listen, speak, read, and write by trial and error and by extensive practical use. Embedded in a whole language approach is the belief that a child's internal motivation is a major contributor to successful acquisition of skills. Therefore, in whole language classrooms considerable emphasis is placed both on practical use of these skills and on building children's motivation and enthusiasm. Communication skills are infused throughout the day as part of lessons in each subject.

How the Debate Misses the Point

We feel strongly that the debate between phonics instruction or a whole language approach misses the point. Unlike whole language, phonics is not a philosophy. Phonics is *not* a method of teaching reading, but rather one of the many strategies readers use to unlock or decode words.[14] Because reading is not about just saying the words, isolated lessons in phonics do not help children become involved readers. Phonics instruction should, however, be part of a program of instruction in reading. The direct teaching of skills is part of an effective whole language approach.

Whole language is based on the understanding that reading is finding the meaning in written language. That's why, for example, you may have noticed that your child can read a word in the context of a familiar book that he or she may not read when the word stands alone. Children develop an awareness of the sounds of our language naturally. This awareness is enhanced or reinforced when a parent or teacher highlights letter sounds for a child, for example, when reading a book together or noticing a sign on a store. Lessons that isolate letter-sound relationships usually go in one ear of the child and out the other. In order for children to remember letter-sound relationships, instruction should be based in something real and personally meaningful to them.

Children should learn phonics as part of many activities based on their individual needs. Different books help children learn particular skills. Some books repeat certain words or phrases, such as *The Gingerbread Man Retold* ("I'll run and run as fast as I can. You can't catch me. I'm the gingerbread man.").[15] Rhyming books or poems help children learn word patterns and sounds. Children are more likely to become enthusiastic readers when they actively read, write, listen to others, and talk about ideas and language. Their interest may be lost if they are required to learn letter sounds as a prerequisite to reading, or spelling as a prerequisite to writing.

What happens when there is an overemphasis on phonics instruction for the whole class? There may be insufficient time for reading interesting literature and talking about the ideas in books. While some children need explicit instruction in order to progress as readers, others may not. Why should everyone in a class have to spend time studying a particular letter and its sounds if some of the children already know how to decipher words? Phonics should be taught, as necessary, during many different reading and writing activities so that children see how to apply these skills in their reading.

Do not be misled by the whole language label or the phonics label. As a parent, you want to know that there is a balance in your child's classroom.[16] If *all* you see and hear about is skills instruction—worksheets on letter sounds, letter of the week, short vowel, long vowel exercises, etc.—you should be concerned. That may mean that little time is devoted to reading books and finding out why these skills are useful.

On the other hand, if your child is reading and writing throughout the day but you don't see any improvement in reading strategies, that may also be a reason for concern. Most children do not learn skills magically. They need to be immersed in interesting reading and writing experiences and also be taught the skills—and not just phonics—needed to read and write.

How Reading Is Taught

Children bring to school a variety of experiences with print. Many can read their own names, recognize street signs and the *M* for McDonald's, and identify different makes of cars or labels on food containers. Your child's reading experiences in school should build from this natural base, using what he or she already knows and adding on from there. A variety of instructional approaches accommodate the learning styles and preferences of all the children in a class and ensure that every child learns to read.

In your child's classroom, look for a balanced approach to teaching reading, one that involves children in exciting reading experiences and teaches them skills as well. Here are the kinds of activities we recommend:

Reading books aloud. One of the best ways to inspire children to become readers is to read to them every day. By listening to good books, children learn that reading is an enjoyable activity. They hear how a competent reader reads, and they learn about different types of literature and different ways to tell a story. They also extend their vocabulary and lengthen their attention spans. Reading aloud is a way to expose children to stimulating books they are not yet able to read on their own. Your child should be read to daily in school.

This example from a third grade class shows how children consolidate their learning after having shared a reading experience. Thinking back to the principles described in Chapter 1, the example also illustrates how learning experiences should be varied and collaborative.

> *The children had just heard their teacher finish reading aloud* Justin and the Best Biscuits in the World *by Mildred Pitts Walter. She asked, "What could we do that would give everyone a chance to show what they liked about this book?" The class brainstormed the following ideas: do a skit, create a mural of scenes, prepare biscuits, make dioramas. They talked about the kinds of ideas they wanted to present. After agreeing on three projects, they divided into groups to plan how they would begin.*

Children respond to books differently and need opportunities to demonstrate what they have learned in a variety of ways—through drama, drawing, cooking, and constructing. All these projects bring children together so they can learn from each other.

Reading books together. The invention of "big books" introduced a new form of reading instruction. Big books have enlarged print that make it possible for a group of children to see the writing and the illustrations and thus "read" the book at the same time. They are effective for teaching specific skills and pointing out patterns, rhymes, or the repetition of sounds.

Some big books have many sight words (words that appear frequently) that your child can learn. Others focus on letter sounds. More fluent readers can work together to study a poem if the teacher writes it on oversized chart paper, thus creating a big book

to meet the needs of a group. The children can analyze the poet's choice of words or how the poem is constructed.

Small reading groups or book clubs. Your child can benefit from meeting in a small group with the teacher several times a week. During this time, children should receive specific instruction based on their needs. These small group times are also wonderful opportunities for children to be part of discussions on a book everyone in the group has read. Based on observations and conferences with children, the teacher can determine what children are ready to learn and can group the class accordingly. Groups should be fluid; they change based on the teacher's assessment of what individual children are ready to learn. Consider what and how your child could learn in this first grade classroom.

> *Several children were seated at a table talking about the story "Spring" in* Frog and Toad Are Friends, *by Arnold Lobel. The teacher commented that Frog and Toad are good friends. She asked the children to think about their friends and how friends help each other. They began to talk about Ralph who fell on the playground yesterday and how they helped him walk back to the classroom. Following this conversation, the children took turns reading from the book. When Maria had difficulty with the word "shutters," they all looked at the picture of the house to figure out what would make the house dark. Max said he has shutters on his house but they are open all the time. The teacher had the children think about the sound 'sh' makes. They found other words in the story that had this sound in them: shining, shouted, and pushed.*

These children know they can bring their own ideas and experiences to a discussion about a book. The teacher applies the principle of making learning meaningful by having children connect their own personal experiences with the words and stories in books.

Independent reading. One of the pleasures of learning to read is having time to relax with a good book. Independent reading time is a chance for children to choose whatever they wish to read—magazines, adventure stories, joke books, sports books, non-fiction books on science or social studies topics—and read on their own or with a partner. Your child should have opportunities for independent reading at school at least several times a week, if not every day. For first graders, the time period may last ten minutes; by third grade the time might be extended to 30 minutes. Children benefit most from independent reading when they have regular conferences with their teacher about their reading.

A classroom filled with interesting print. Print should be evident throughout the classroom. Look for this kind of variety in your child's classroom: labels for materials, attendance charts, job charts, the daily schedule, a morning message to the children, a message board, charts about topics of study, enlarged poems, or signs to remind children of rules and procedures for the classroom.

Questions about Golden Gate Park

1. How big is it?
2. Is it the biggest park in San Francisco?
3. Who owns the park?
4. What did it look like a long time ago?
5. How do you grow grass? How long does it take to grow grass?
6. Is there a place to eat in the park?
7. How many rats are in the park?
8. How many playgrounds are there?
9. Who built Golden Gate Park?

Integrating reading in other content areas. Because learning to read and using reading to learn is so important, instruction should take place throughout the day, not just at designated reading times. Reading skills can be taught—sometimes to the whole class, to small groups, or one-on-one—as part of many activities throughout the day. For example, if the class is learning a new song and the teacher writes the words on a big chart, children can read them like a big book. Children practice reading as they read the daily schedule, the rules for using the computer, or the directions for cleaning up the art area.

Look for many different kinds of reading activities in your child's classroom as well as instruction in particular skills. The goal is for your child to become competent as a beginning reader and to learn to love reading.

How Parents Can Help

- Read aloud to your child as often as possible, every day if you can—enjoying books together does more to help your child become a good reader than anything else you can do.

- Set aside a time for your child to read aloud to you—select books that are easy to read so your child can feel successful.

- Resist the urge to ask your child to always "sound out" an unknown word every time he or she stumbles. Talk about what might make sense based on the rest of the sentence or skip it and come back to it later. If you noticed that your child read that word on another page, find it together. Or just tell your child the word. After all, the most important thing is that reading together be a pleasant experience.

- Talk about the books you and your child have read—share what you like (or don't like), compare your opinions of the characters, or think about a time you did something similar to what you have read.

- Encourage your child to read the print that surrounds you in everyday life—signs, directions, labels, addresses, the telephone book, messages on television, and the newspaper.

- Write messages to your child—a brief note in the lunch box saying "I love you!" or "Have fun playing soccer at recess today."

Questions to Ask Your Child's Teacher

- Could you show me an example of a book my child reads easily?

- What type of book is my child working on now?

- What kinds of activities related to reading does my child like to do—drawing, writing, acting…?

- What are your goals for my child in reading and how will you help him achieve these goals? What can I do to help?

- Which reading strategies does my child use most confidently?

- Does my child choose to read during free time?

- Does my child participate in discussions about what she reads in school?

- What have been her favorite read aloud books?

- Are there particular poems or songs that my child likes?

– 4 –
How Children
Become Writers

"Mom, I need your recipe for cupcakes. You know, the one with the M&Ms in the icing? We're writing books about how to do things and I want to write about how to make those cupcakes. I'm also writing a book with Carla on Rollerblading because we're both really good at it."

Children develop as writers when they feel that they have something important to say and they believe that their thoughts and experiences are worth recording. In the classroom, your child needs to write during many different activities and on a variety of topics. School writing experiences should offer children a choice of topics that build on their naturally developing interests. Once children recognize the power of writing, they are motivated to learn the necessary skills.

The process of learning how to write begins at a very early age. Young children, using crayons or markers, write with great enthusiasm and eagerness. Toddlers and preschoolers think that all they have to do is pick up a pen and scrawl little lines and dots. Gradually, they realize that writing is speech in the form of symbols on paper, so they talk and scribble away—and expect you to read this scribble! As their fine motor skills develop, children draw pictures and dictate words to accompany the pictures. Sometimes they try to write words. They may start with words they remember seeing somewhere, or they may attempt to write the sounds they hear when they say the words aloud. For example, a child might write "D" or "DG" for "DOG."

From these modest but enthusiastic beginnings, writers emerge. Children who have been encouraged to express their ideas on paper from an early age become confident about their ability to write. The more they write, the more they learn about writing. Your child's writing experiences in school should build on this natural momentum rather than imposing premature or excessive demands for correct spelling, punctuation, and other mechanics. Children who are enthusiastic about writing will learn the mechanics as they strive to put their ideas into print.

What's Involved in Learning to Write

Children need to learn that writing is putting ideas into print.
Writers have to think about what they want to say, find the words to represent their ideas, and put the words on paper so that they can be read and understood. The example that follows illustrates this in action. As you read it, consider how many principles of effective learning the teacher has employed.

Hector and Taylor, two baseball enthusiasts, had been having a heated argument. They disagreed about which combination of baseball players would make the best team. The teacher encouraged each of them to use this argument as a basis for their next writing project. Hector began by listing his ideas for teams and explaining his choices, including each player's merits and weaknesses. Taylor decided to first describe the characteristics of a good team.

Children grow as writers in classrooms when assignments capitalize on their interests. Writing helps children clarify their thinking because they have to ask themselves, "What message do I want to send? What can I do to make sure that others can understand my message?"

Children grow as writers when they write about their own life experiences and ideas. Just as established authors use familiar material in their writing, children feel most comfortable about writing when they can write on topics they know about best. Their interest in writing is stimulated when assignments begin with something personal. A teacher began a writing lesson with second graders by telling them a personal story.

> *"Do you see this bandage on my chin? I was taking out the garbage after dinner yesterday evening. It was cold and windy and the path to my house was covered with ice. I slipped on the ice and hit my chin on the garbage can. My chin began to bleed. I went inside and my daughter helped me clean the cut and put on a bandage." The teacher then asked if anyone had a story to tell related to the winter weather. Children began telling stories about falling on the ice, getting stuck in cars, having frozen pipes, and what they did when school was closed. After sharing their stories aloud, the children went off to write, while the teacher talked with two children who were not sure they had story ideas yet.*

Children need to learn many skills to become writers. Once children have brainstormed ideas, they have to consider how to convey the story or message. Writing requires a complex set of skills. Some of the skills they need are creative; others are mechanical.

These skills include:

- choosing a topic

- sequencing ideas

- conveying an idea clearly

- organizing information or the story line

- using mechanics correctly (spelling, punctuation, capitalization)

- editing and revising

- proofreading

To be good writers, children need many opportunities to write for different purposes. Many of us can recall sitting in school facing a blank piece of paper and having nothing to write about. Your child should not have to repeat this unhappy experience. Writing should be integrated into classroom life. The following are some examples:

- writing personal reflections in their journals

- developing stories about everyday events—a new pet, a flat tire, a trip to visit relatives

- observing, explaining, or describing processes in their math logs or science journals

- writing reactions to books in their reading logs

- writing research or book reports

- creating math word problems

- participating in group writing projects (such as skits or plays related to books they have read)

- making signs, labels, rules, game instructions, programs, invitations, letters, and so forth

- using a word processing program on the computer

With numerous opportunities to write for various purposes, children discover that writing serves many functions.

How Writing Is Taught

Research shows that the most effective way to teach young children to be good writers is to emphasize what they can do, and gradually teach them the skills they need to write in conventional ways.[17] Because children today are doing all kinds of writing before they can master the mechanics, they need to hear these messages: "We are all authors who have important ideas to communicate. I really want to know what you have to say." By writing, children gradually learn to think about what they want to say and how to go about organizing and expressing their ideas in ways that can be understood by others.

Learning to read and learning to write go hand in hand. Therefore, children in the primary grades benefit from learning the two simultaneously. As children become more proficient readers, they notice the conventions of print—that is, the commonly accepted ways to spell, punctuate, and organize their writing. Children who are writers notice how authors carefully craft their books. Opportunities to read and listen to varied and interesting literature help children become better writers.

Learning the Mechanics of Writing

Children should learn the mechanics, such as spelling, handwriting, and grammar (e.g., punctuation and use of capital letters) in the process of writing. This way of teaching the mechanics may not be what you experienced in school. You may have practiced spelling, handwriting, and punctuation in isolated lessons *before* you began writing stories. But, premature emphasis on the mechanics can become roadblocks to writing. When mechanics are taught and practiced in the context of children writing, children are motivated to learn and use them because they have an audience and a story to tell.

For instance, as children write they are encouraged to listen to the sounds they hear in a given word and spell that word the way it sounds. In other words, they use letter sounds or phonics to do their best to spell. With this approach, their initial writing efforts aren't inhibited by an inability to spell a word correctly. A class of twenty-five to thirty children can all get their ideas down on paper without struggling over spelling or being overly dependent on the teacher.

Many parents wonder how children will learn to spell words correctly if they are encouraged to write without attending to accurate spelling. Remember how your child first began to talk. There was lots of babbling before recognizable words were clear. When children spell a word the way it sounds to them, the process is called writing with invented spelling. Using "invented spelling" is an important step on the road to becoming a writer and learning standard spelling. Once children can get some semblance of a word on paper (which can occur as early as preschool or kindergarten), they can begin to grasp that spelling is standardized. Young writers may not hear or use all the letters.

Children progress through developmental stages as they learn to spell. By working on reading skills and by analyzing children's writing, teachers can provide children with appropriate spelling instruction. For example, children usually begin by using consonants first because the sounds are more distinct than vowel sounds. They may write a whole sentence using letters that represent the initial sounds of words, for example, "I l m c" for "I love my cat." Later, they add ending sounds, so the word cat looks like "ct."

Children will begin using vowels after they understand that the sounds between consonants are represented by letters. Figuring out which vowel to use can be complicated because vowel sounds are more subtle than consonant sounds. It is much easier to remember the difference between the sounds of 'b' and 'd' than it is to distinguish between the 'ah' sound of 'a' as in bat and the 'eh' sound of 'e' as in bet.

Most children also need explicit directions in learning to spell words accurately. First graders who write extensively can be held accountable for a list of basic words that they use regularly. Second and third graders can begin to memorize spelling rules and patterns, core lists of words, specific words from their writing, and play spelling games. Research shows that children who write more use more interesting language and are better spellers.[18]

Proper handwriting is another mechanical skill children learn in time. In the primary grades, children's fine motor skills are still developing. For some children, learning to form letters correctly and efficiently is a difficult task. Children should usually practice handwriting in the context of an ongoing writing program. Eventually, most children realize their writing can more easily be read if their handwriting is legible. At that point, they are more willing to work on their handwriting so others can read it.

Another aspect of the mechanics of writing are actions such as putting spaces between words, using capital letters, and using punctuation correctly. Children are able to learn these skills and use them in their writing only if teachers create meaningful opportunities for them to do so. For instance, children can be encouraged to read their work aloud to hear where the punctuation belongs and add it. They can also be asked to notice where a word has been inadvertently left out. As they watch their teacher writing on a chart, they can see the various conventions of print as the teacher calls attention to them.

Learning to Be Writers

While daily opportunities to write are essential, three or more discrete periods during each week should be devoted specifically to developing writing skills. Scheduled writing times allow children to focus on what they want to say and how to say it. This special time is often called "writing workshop." It is designed to give children regular experiences with writing so they come to see themselves as authors. Hence, during writing workshop, children make decisions about their work. They are given choices of topics and are allowed to develop their ideas creatively.[19]

The elements of a typical writing workshop are the mini-lesson, writing time, conferences, sharing, revising and editing, and publishing. Following is a discussion of each element of a writing workshop based on our personal classroom experiences and the many classrooms we have visited.

Mini-Lessons. Before a formal writing time, children benefit from a brief lesson. The teacher may select a specific aspect of writing based upon his or her observations of the children's work. Sometimes teachers may read a part of a story to illustrate a point and generate class discussion. For example, we find that effective teachers often read the beginning of a story to stimulate a class discussion about how authors begin stories, create moods, or describe settings.

> *The teacher read several passages from different books to show how authors describe a setting. The class talked about how one author lists the particular objects located in the setting while another uses descriptive language, setting a tone which makes the place seem scary. The teacher and children together created a chart of the different ways to develop a story setting. They posted the chart in the classroom and the teacher encouraged the children to add to it whenever someone notices a different author's technique.*

Other mini-lesson topics might relate to the mechanics of writing, such as use of periods, capital letters, or the structure of paragraphs. For example, Monday the children would examine the different ways writers end a sentence (period, question mark, or exclamation point). On Tuesday, the children could search together for periods, question marks, and exclamation points in a book. On Wednesday, a child who has used these marks in a story she has written shares part of it. These mini-lessons are small doses of instruction that children can absorb. In addition, children are more likely to try out new concepts or skills eagerly when skill instruction relates to their own writing and comes just before writing time.

Just as children benefit from small group instruction in reading, they will make more progress as writers if instruction is individualized. In other words, the skills they are taught are based on the teacher's assessments and evaluation of each child's actual writing. So, in addition to large group instruction, your child should also receive small group instruction focusing on a particular skill, such as the rules for using capital letters or analyzing sequencing the beginning, middle, and end of a story. Each child should also have individual attention from the teacher during conferences which are discussed below.

Writing Time. Following the lesson, children try out what they have learned. They need to work on their own, but occasionally they may want to write with a friend. Young children often begin by drawing a picture. They then write words to go with it. As children progress as writers, they may plan their story by talking about it. Gradually, children do more and more of their planning mentally. Some children like to talk and exchange ideas as they write. Other children have difficulty concentrating with too much talking around them. Teachers can address these differences by having some quiet time during writing workshop.

Conferences. During the writing time, children need opportunities to confer individually with the teacher to discuss their work or to learn a specific skill. Even just a few minutes of undivided attention from the teacher, when questions are answered, progress noted, or advice

given, can build children's confidence and writing skills. The issues that emerge from these conferences can be the basis for lessons for small groups and the entire class.

Sharing. Children's writing improves when they can read their drafts to the class and ask for help in specific areas, such as finding an idea for a good title or a better opening sentence. This process of sharing allows children to appreciate each other's work and to give and receive constructive criticism. Children can also read finished pieces as a way to celebrate their accomplishments.

Revising and Editing. As children progress as writers, they are ready to learn to revise and edit their work. Revision may include adding or deleting information, rearranging sentences, or making other changes. This process can seem overwhelming or disheartening to a beginning writer. For this reason we encourage teachers to focus on only one or two things at a time in a child's story. For example, considering a new beginning to a story is one way to start; another is elaborating an idea in the story. Editing may include correcting mechanical errors. Children could be asked to find one or two mechanical errors by first looking over their stories to see if each sentence begins with a capital letter or ends with an appropriate punctuation mark. If your child is focusing on one skill at a time in this way, the work you see may still contain errors, so find out the teacher's system and look for progress over time.

Publishing. Once children have had some experience revising and editing their work, they are ready to think about putting it in a form for others to see. They should know that this process is the equivalent of "publishing," that is, putting their writing on display for others to read. As children gain experience as writers they can begin to do more editing and rewriting to get their writing ready to be "published." Learning that publishing companies have editors who do a final check before a book is published will help them see the teacher as the "final" editor in their classroom. For many first graders, too much revision is unreasonable—getting their thoughts on paper is challenge enough. Second and third graders can rewrite some of their "to-be-published" writing or type it on the computer where they learn to use a spell checker. Many teachers welcome the help of parents for typing children's edited stories so children don't spend endless amounts of time recopying their work.

Integrating Writing in Other Content Areas

Children benefit from many opportunities to write and think about writing throughout the day. These opportunities should be part of their ongoing work in the classroom. For instance, during a class discussion about the computer, your child might suggest that the user instructions have to be updated because the new computer uses a different kind of disk. This is a perfect opportunity for a few children to work together to write new instructions and bring them to a class meeting to see if they make sense. On another occasion children might like to compare how different authors use

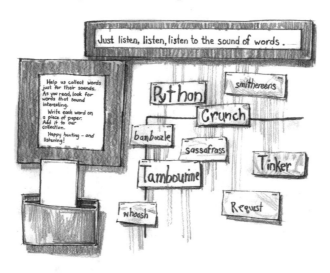

descriptive language to create a mood or collect words that have interesting sounds.

When children are viewed as emerging writers, whose ideas can be encouraged using whatever skills they currently possess, they can work on writing in many different ways during the course of each day at school and at home. The more varied the opportunities to write and learn the mechanics of writing, the more likely it is that your child will learn to be an accomplished writer.

How Parents Can Help

- Write letters and thank you notes together—begin by having your child dictate, later copy what you write, and then rewrite with your help.

- Make shopping lists together—group items by categories and have your child suggest ideas.

- When interesting or funny things happen, talk with your child about how you could write stories about these events—begin by saying the first line, have your child say the next, and keep alternating until you have finished the story.

- Put up a message board so family members can write messages to each other.

- Give your child a diary or a calendar with space to write a word or two about what happened each day.

- Invite your child to write captions for pictures in a family photo album.

Questions to Ask Your Child's Teacher

- Can you show me samples of my child's writing from the beginning of the year and now?

- What kinds of writing does he most enjoy?

- Can you tell me about the progression of her spelling skills?

- What does he do when he doesn't know how to spell a word?

- Does my child write as a free choice activity, such as writing skits or game directions?

- What are your goals for my child as a writer this year?

- How will you help her achieve these goals?

- What can I do to help?

– 5 –
How Children Become Mathematical Thinkers

"I've got a homework project that's going to take all week. See this chart? I have to write down when I go to sleep, when I wake up, how long it takes me to brush my teeth, eat dinner, and when I watch TV. We're collecting data. We're trying to figure out how we spend our days and how much sleep we get on school nights."

Mathematical thinking is organizing information, comparing quantities, and seeing relationships. Learning the concepts and language of mathematics—more, less, equal, a fraction of, multiples of, and so on—helps children to plan, calculate, reason, and communicate solutions to problems. To think mathematically, children need to go well beyond basic computation skills. They need opportunities in school to develop an understanding of mathematics by applying skills to real problems.

When you were in elementary school, the focus of the math curriculum probably was not "mathematical thinking" but rather "arithmetic." You were most likely taught number facts ($3 + 4 = 7$ or $7 \times 8 = 56$) and basic operations ($+ - \times \div$). Students who knew their facts and could add, subtract, multiply, and divide quickly were successful in math. The world our children are growing up in places greater emphasis on knowing how to *apply* mathematical concepts to new problems. As a result, children must learn to think mathematically. You will see, as you read this chapter, that we're not saying children don't need to learn arithmetic. They do. But mathematical thinking includes much more.

How Children Learn to Think Mathematically

In our adult lives, we use mathematical thinking all the time. We calculate when to leave for the movie theater, considering how long it takes to get there, about how long it will take to find a place to park, and whether we think there will be a line for tickets. If we want a new kitchen floor, we have to decide which floor tiles we can afford, given the size of the room and the number of tiles we need. In analyzing a project at work, we consider whether a spreadsheet will show the information clearly, or if a narrative explanation is sufficient.

According to the National Council of Teachers of Mathematics (NCTM)[20], to become effective mathematical thinkers, students must learn about:

- patterns and relationships

- number concepts and operations

- estimation

- geometry and spatial relationships

- measurement

- probability and statistics

These components form the basis for mathematics instruction. In every grade, your child should have opportunities to explore each of these areas.

The study of ***patterns and relationships*** helps children think about connections between objects and events. Patterns and relationships are essential to understanding our number system, ordering information, and predicting results in fields such as science and economics. What is the same and different about groups of objects, events, or numbers? What comes next or in between? How are numbers, objects, and events linked? To answer questions such as these, children in the primary grades learn the following skills:

- studying characteristics or attributes of objects such as shape, size, and color

- sorting and classifying numbers and objects

- recognizing, creating, copying, and extending patterns

- using language to describe and compare relationships (more than, less than, the same as)

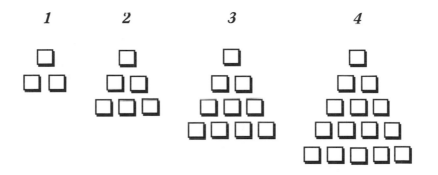

Number concepts are the meanings attached to number symbols. For instance, 3 stands for three objects; the three in the number 35 means thirty; and in 1.3, three tenths. *Number operations* are the basic arithmetic procedures of addition, subtraction, multiplication, and division. We use number concepts and operations daily in our everyday world to count, measure, describe, locate, and identify objects. Children in the primary grades learn number concepts and operations by:

- building physical models to explore place value (ones, tens, hundreds, thousands, etc.), counting, and grouping

- reading, writing, and comparing numbers

- solving problems "in their heads" instead of using paper and pencil

- adding, subtracting, multiplying, and dividing numbers on paper, and learning the steps and reasons for each operation

- using a calculator

Estimation is the ability to make a sensible guess to answer a mathematical question. How many people attended the party? What is the cost of a gallon of milk? How far do you live from the center of the city? Answers to these questions involve number, value, distance, and time—all mathematical concepts. Knowing how to estimate is essential because quantitative and spatial problems arise continually in everyday life. Sometimes reasonable estimates rather than exact answers are the most useful solutions to problems. Primary grade activities that promote estimating skills are:

- using strategies to figure out the number of objects in a container

- choosing a tool to measure a certain space or object

- approximating the answer to questions such as "How much?" "How long?" "How much time or money?" and "How heavy?"

Geometry and spatial relationships means exploring the qualities of two- and three-dimensional objects (e.g., triangles, rectangles, cubes, pyramids). Just as activities with numbers, patterns, and estimation help children see relationships and solve problems, experiences with geometric concepts and skills help children to develop an appreciation and understanding of our geometric world and describe it in an orderly way. Geometric understandings are developed by:

- classifying and comparing shapes

- building two- and three-dimensional constructions

- writing and talking about how shapes can be combined, moved or rearranged, changed in size, and divided into smaller parts

Measurement is the study of attributes such as length, capacity, weight, mass, area, volume, time, temperature, and angle. We use measurement skills and select appropriate tools daily. Studying measurement, children address questions such as "How long?" "How heavy?" "Which holds more?" "How long will this take?" "How much will this cost?" They do this by:

- estimating and measuring objects

- choosing the appropriate tools (ruler, meter stick, scale, measuring cup, timer, etc.)

- telling time and making judgments about the passage of time

- recognizing and counting coins and bills and making change

Probability and statistics involves determining whether something is likely to happen and why. Both probability and statistics organize and describe information in graphs that can be easily interpreted. With more and more statistical information in our daily lives, we are regularly called upon to make decisions and predictions. To make good decisions, we have to understand what the information tells us. Activities that help children learn about probability and statistics include:

- collecting, describing, and recording data

- creating, reading, and drawing conclusions using graphs and charts

- making predictions based on data

How Math Is Taught

Problem solving is the core of mathematical thinking. Correct answers to problems are important, so learning calculating skills is necessary, but problem solving emphasizes the process of getting there. While learning computational skills, your child also needs opportunities to solve mathematical problems and develop strategies for reaching and evaluating solutions. Children should learn to:

- state a problem in their own words

- identify what is needed to solve the problem

- try out different methods

- recall similar problems and use familiar skills

- ask themselves if their answers make sense, and, if necessary, try again

The key to a good math program for your child is finding the right balance. A program can emphasize problem solving while children still learn computation skills. For example, if a child gets the wrong answer to a problem and there is no discussion of how he or she approached the problem, then there is too much focus on answers alone. However, a program where process is emphasized but accuracy of answers is ignored is also out of balance. In addition, programs have to recognize that children approach learning in different ways. One child may memorize math facts easily and compute quickly. Another child may never achieve quick recall or may consistently rely on slow, deliberate calculations to find answers. Both children can become mathematical thinkers.

Using Math Materials

There are many ways that children use concrete materials to explore mathematical ideas. The following explanations and anecdotes illustrate some ways children do this.

Children in a first grade classroom can learn number facts while using materials to actively explore the meaning of numbers. The children in this class were ready to extend their learning and were given appropriate opportunities to do so.

Several groups of children were at work—some with Cuisenaire rods, others with unifix cubes.[21] *They had been challenged to find as many ways to "build 10" as they could. Some children proceeded systematically: 9+1, 8+2, 7+3, 6+4, 5+5. Others tried random combinations. One child decided to try something else: 3+4+3, 2+5+3, 1+6+3. Many children built and others recorded the findings. Later everyone compared their records of how they had solved this problem.*

In a second grade classroom children can learn geometry by constructing different shapes. They work with geoboards—wooden or plastic squares with nails placed at regular intervals. Children use the boards to form shapes by stretching rubberbands around the nails. These same materials could be used by third graders to solve problems of perimeter and area.

Because children have different levels of knowledge about shapes, classroom experiences should challenge children by letting them work at their own levels.

Each pair of children had a geoboard and rubberbands. The teacher discussed the materials and how to use them carefully. She assigned the following: "Work with your partner to see how many different shapes you can make. Keep a record of the shapes you make in your math log.[22] You may draw your shapes using the geodot paper[23] if you wish or write descriptions of your shapes."

A lesson such as this encourages children who are familiar with simple shapes to create more complex ones. It also encourages your child to stretch his or her thinking (what we used to call "doing extra work"). Consider as well how this activity demonstrated learning as a shared responsibility, with both teacher and children taking initiative. Let's see what happened next.

After working with the geoboards, children presented their findings to the rest of the group. They commented about their constructions and compared their shapes to those made by others. As children used names to describe the shapes, the teacher recorded them on chart paper. They asked interesting questions, for instance, "Is a triangle still a triangle if it's turned upside down?" For homework, the teacher told the children to write their own definition of a triangle in their math logs.

Children clarify their thinking by talking, drawing, and writing about what they are doing. The homework assignment reinforces the lesson.

Using Calculators and Computers

Calculators and computers are part of the everyday equipment in most classrooms today. Some of you may worry that children who use these tools before they have learned basic computation skills will never learn how to compute.

Although calculators don't replace the need for computation, they have many advantages. Calculators allow children to compute with large numbers easily, to check their answers, and to work on solving complicated problems. Just as with other tools, lots of experiences with calculators enable young children to learn about when a particular tool is the most efficient way to solve a problem.

Children can use computers to construct graphs, explore patterns, create and experiment with geometric shapes and relationships, practice computation, and play math games. Neither calculators or computers have the ability to think. They are tools to assist children's mathematical thinking.

Math Throughout the Day

Your child will learn more if mathematical thinking is encouraged throughout the day. During class meetings, for example, mathematical thinking happens as teachers and children:

- discuss the daily calendar

- review the sequences in the day's or week's schedule

- graph the weather or temperature

- use a time line to count the number of days spent in school

- talk about the time of day or how much time there is before something else happens

- estimate how long it will take to do something or go somewhere

Mathematical questions and problems often arise naturally in other areas of study, for instance, in social studies. As children investigate topics, they have many opportunities to apply math skills as part of their research activities as illustrated in this first grade teacher's classroom.

The children were studying their neighborhood in social studies. With clipboards and pencils in hand, they counted the stores, buildings, fire hydrants, windows, and trees in the area and recorded their findings. To simplify their recording, the teacher showed them how to keep a tally: ᅡᅡᅡᅡ.

At another time they made graphs to show different forms of transportation. When they got ready to build a model of the neighborhood in the classroom, the teacher discussed the relative sizes of buildings and cars so they could decide which size milk cartons were needed to construct particular buildings. During the second month of the study, they set up a store similar to one in the neighborhood, and "bought and sold" goods.

There are many ways to connect learning across subject areas. In the following example, notice how a teacher relates math to physical education.

The third graders were working hard with the physical education teacher to improve their fitness scores. Their teacher helped them create a chart to record their times and distances and the number of sit ups they did. At the end of the second week they decided to make personal graphs of their progress and a class graph, too.

Requirements for mathematical thinking crop up regularly in the everyday life of the classroom. The most effective instruction in math takes advantage of children's naturally occurring experiences. They explore interesting problems using important mathematical ideas.

How Parents Can Help

- Play games together—dice games, board games such as Monopoly, and card games.

- Plan aloud with your child before you go on errands— ask, "What do we need to bring?...Where should we go first...next...last?"

- Talk about time: "It's half an hour (or 30 minutes) until dinner."

- Have a clock at home with numbers and hands (analog), not just digital. Then play games, closing your eyes, and seeing if you can predict when 10, or 30, or 60 seconds passes.

- Involve your child in shopping for groceries and handling small amounts of money.

- Give your child a personal calendar or create one on the computer—together mark down recent events and cross off the days.

- Encourage your child's interest in building with different kinds of blocks, or making things out of "junk."

- Record your child's height in inches and meters on a door, tape, or wall chart.

- Read the weather page together or watch the Weather Channel. Talk about the predictions and how much the temperature will change.

Questions to Ask Your Child's Teacher

- What are your goals for my child this year in math?

- How will I know she is making good progress?

- What kinds of problems does my child like to solve?

- How does he approach new problems?

- Can you show me some examples of how she goes about solving problems?

- What strategies does she use to add or subtract large numbers?

- Can you tell me about his progress in learning basic number facts?

- What can I do to help?

– 6 –
How Children Learn Social Studies

"Guess what? We're doing an investigation about places that sell food. We're going to find out what each family eats and where they buy food and also how often people go to McDonald's and Burger King and places like that. Don't we shop at two different big supermarkets? That's what I said at school today. But don't we also go to the store on the corner where Jim is the manager?"

Social studies is the study of people–how people live, work, get along with others, solve problems, shape, and are shaped by their surroundings. Children learn social studies by exploring the world around them. In the example above, children study the stores in their neighborhood in order to learn about the work people do, where foods come from, and how they are transported. Children living in a farming community might study the same concepts but in a very different setting. The content of the social studies curriculum should allow your child to explore important concepts and learn how to do research.

You, like us, may remember social studies as memorizing facts about crops and industries in each state, important dates from the American Revolution, and the names of state capitals. (And, it's likely that most of us have forgotten what we learned!) Because young children build knowledge by connecting new information to what they already know, we strongly believe that social studies investigations in the primary grades should start with your child's everyday experiences in the world and build outward from there.

What's Involved in Social Studies

Some people advocate that young children should begin to learn a core of knowledge in first, second, and third grades—world geography, world and American civilization, and history. While we agree that this knowledge is an important part of children's education, our experience and child development research tell us that when concepts and ideas are too far removed from a child's first-hand experience they have little meaning. Information that is memorized without purpose or significance has no lasting value. Children have to be able to build on what they know and connect new information to the familiar. In this way when they learn factual information, they begin to see patterns and make sense of what is unfamiliar. Your child lives in an age where information is constantly changing. To prepare for a professional life in the 21st Century, your child has to learn how to think, ask questions, find information, and solve problems, not just memorize facts.

That is why we believe that primary grade children should explore social studies first using experiences right in their immediate environment. They can learn more about maps by making maps of their rooms at home or their classroom, their school, and their neighborhood, than by looking at maps of the world. Before studying American or world history, they can study their families, communities, towns, or cities to learn about how people function in groups and communities. Social studies instruction should build on children's natural curiosity to explore the world around them.

Learning Social Studies Concepts

No matter what the specific content is, there are several big ideas or concepts that organize the discipline of social studies. Once children gain understanding of these concepts in relation to their own immediate experience, they can draw on and apply these same concepts to studies of the larger world. For children in the early grades, the big concepts of social studies can be grouped under six headings:

- basic human needs
- human similarities and differences
- human interdependence
- rights and responsibilities
- people and the places they live
- people and the past

Children can learn about **basic human needs** by first examining their own actions and then gradually researching how their families and other community members live. They begin to see that basic physical and social needs—safety, security, food, clothing, and shelter—are consistent among all people, regardless of when and where they live. As they get older, children can compare their actions and behaviors in daily living to those of people who lived long ago and those who live in more distant places. They learn that basic needs are universal, but the ways different people meet these needs vary.

To learn about **human similarities and differences** children can share information about themselves and listen to what others have to say. Helping children to understand human diversity includes creating opportunities for them to see events and ideas from the perspective of others. They discover differences in the size and composition of families, the types of houses people live in, what they eat, the kinds of work they do, the ways they express emotions, and the roles and responsibilities of children. Learning about similarities and differences helps children recognize and appreciate diversity in thinking, feeling, and acting, and promotes understanding of the many different influences that shape people's lives.

The concept of **human interdependence** includes understanding how people depend on others to accomplish tasks, how they divide labor and share responsibility, and how they exchange goods and services. As children explore how goods are produced and services performed, they learn about the world of work and acquire an appreciation for the different jobs people perform.

For children in the primary grades, **rights and responsibilities**—fairness, individual rights, and adhering to rules—are issues of great significance. As their sense of justice and fairness grows, they are ready to consider the reasons for establishing rules and the role of government in society.

Examining **people and the places they live** leads children to understand how people's lives are shaped by their physical environment. This is the study of geography. They explore concepts such as the following:

- How do the physical features of our location affect our lives?

- How does climate affect how people live?

- In what ways do the natural resources that are available in a particular locale influence the types of houses people build and the foods they eat?

History, or what we call **people and the past** has meaning for children when they have first-hand opportunities to examine their own personal life histories. Some ways your child might do this are by writing about memories of being younger, making a family scrapbook, or constructing a personal time line. Interviewing family members about their childhoods also leads children to historical understanding.

Children can study many different topics or content areas to gain understanding of these big concepts. In our work with teachers we purposefully refer to topics as "studies" for two reasons. First, the word "studies" connotes active research and in-depth pursuit of a topic. Second, through studies children have opportunities to be challenged by subject matter. Your child's teacher may also refer to these as "themes" or "units." Whatever the name, from our perspective, the defining characteristic of a worthwhile study is richness. For example, a study of "Food: From Origin to Table" is "rich" because it lends itself to many different kinds of first-hand investigations. The topic of study should be based on what children can explore directly in their immediate environment. We have seen children in Alaska studying ice fishing and children in a Vermont town (with several covered bridges) studying *Roads and Bridges: Who and What Travels on Them.*

The same general topic can be approached in different ways, depending upon the age of the children. For example, if the topic is families, most first graders are interested in themselves and their families. They want to know what their families eat, where their families shop, and what jobs their family members do. As children get older their interests extend to the larger community. A study of families for third graders might involve learning about immigration, expanding children's thinking beyond their own experience into other time periods and other places.

Learning Social Studies Skills

In social studies, your child should learn skills—primarily research and critical thinking skills—along with content. This can happen in classrooms where children study topics that provide opportunities for first-hand investigations. A good study topic leads children to ask questions, actively investigate issues, and make connections between what they are learning and their daily lives.

Imagine for a moment that your child is in a first grade class studying families. Your child brings family photographs from home to school, the class discusses their families, and they read stories and poetry about families. All of the children write letters inviting you and other family members to be interviewed about where you grew up and the kinds of work you do. Among other activities, the children draw and paint family portraits, create family trees, design maps and blueprints of their homes, and make graphs about numbers of people living in their household. Think of the many skills as well as facts and concepts your child can learn in the process of this intensive study.

By studying their own families, children learn about the size and configurations of families, how family members earn a living, the roles of family members today and in the past, and family customs, such as those related to foods and holidays. They also practice skills of locating information, comparing and contrasting, and drawing conclusions.

We observed a second grade teacher use a study of the community to help children learn important concepts and skills. This was just a small segment of the action.

The class was studying their community and the buildings in it. They began the study by identifying as many different kinds of buildings as they could in their neighborhood—stores, offices, library, school, firehouse, gas station, recreation center, and houses. They developed a list of questions related to the buildings; for example, who lives or works in the building; what special equipment is in the building; what does the building look like. They planned a trip to several of the buildings to get answers to their questions. Following the trip, the children talked about what they observed. Some children decided to build a model of a building, others painted pictures of buildings, and still others designed a map to show where the buildings were located. A few children went to the library to find books about the history of their town.

By studying a topic in the immediate environment, children learn about their community and the people in it. During the course of their investigation they practice skills such as generating questions, using primary sources (field trip observations), and putting information together in pictures, maps, and models. All of the principles that make learning effective described in Chapter 1 were evident in this project.

- The children study their own community *(meaningful learning)*.
- They take trips to visit buildings *(active learning)*.
- They explore questions in depth, over time, and pursue special interests *(challenging learning)*.
- There is diversity in the products the children produce *(varied learning)*.
- Children work together on projects related to the study *(collaborative learning)*.
- Children think about what they want to learn and decide how to demonstrate their learning *(shared responsibility)*.

Keeping these principles in mind can help you evaluate your child's social studies instruction. The highest priority for a good program is relevance. Is the content being studied helping your child to make personal, meaningful connections to the world around her? For example, if your child is studying a distant culture such as China or India, do you have the sense that the teacher is providing opportunities for your child to link what is being learned to her life—herself, her family, her community? These linkages are what make social studies learning meaningful for children.

Although we have stated that active learning is an important principle, by itself active learning does not guarantee a good social studies program. The activities children do must be connected to the important social studies concepts. As you evaluate your child's social studies program, question whether active projects such as weaving, cooking, or pottery making are linked to learning concepts such as basic human needs or human interdependence.

How Social Studies Is Taught

Most schools have a social studies curriculum that outlines the areas of study or content for each grade. Your child's teacher can usually choose how to address these topics. There are two effective ways your child can be supported in learning the big ideas or concepts related to social studies and the research and critical thinking skills. One is by exploring a topic over time as part of a long term study incorporating research. The second is by participating in a classroom community where children experience social studies concepts first hand.

Long Term Studies and Research

Many topics lend themselves to long term study and research. For example, we helped a teacher design a study of communication that allowed children to study a topic in depth and to do extensive research over time. At the same time, the topic helped children to gain insight into many important social studies concepts. The chart on the next page displays the kinds of activities second graders did as they studied communication and how these activities related to the essential concepts of social studies.

Communication Study

Concepts	Activities or Explorations
basic human needs	• Identified ways to call for emergency help. • Discussed ways that people in their family and community communicate needs and feelings. • Compared their needs with those of people in the past and in other places. Described differences in communicating needs.
human similarities and differences	• Interviewed family members and collected data about how they communicate with others (telephone, letters, faxes, e-mail). • Compared today's methods of communication with those used in the past.
human interdependence	• Studied local work places (telephone company, radio station, post office, neighborhood newspaper). • Interviewed communication workers who described their jobs during a classroom visit. • Investigated communication systems used in the school (intercom, mailboxes, messengers).
rights and responsibilities	• Reviewed classroom rules for discussions. • Discussed rules for public and private communication. • Discussed the concept of "freedom of speech."
people and the places they live	• Compared newspapers from different cities. • Studied the use of beepers and cellular phones. • Visited a telephone company, local newspaper, radio station, post office.
people and the past	• Researched inventions related to communication. (e.g., library, Internet, CD-ROM) • Investigated communication methods parents and older family members used as children.

By participating in these activities, children explored communication in relation to themselves, their families, and their local community. Some children wrote and broadcast a weekly radio show on the school's intercom system; others published a weekly newspaper. And still others connected with pen pals around the world via the Internet. As children investigated these options, they learned about their community and how it functions. They had opportunities to ask many "why" and "how" questions about their own daily lives.

Learning Social Studies in a Classroom Community

The ability to function in a democratic community citizenship—is an important component of the social studies curriculum. When the classroom functions as a community, children practice responsible citizenship on a day-to-day basis. They make choices, learn to accept different points of view and different ways of thinking, and are encouraged to treat others with respect. Your child's experience in a classroom community should provide a daily environment where all individuals have rights and responsibilities, where each child contributes to the well-being of others, and at the same time is able to express and feel proud of his or her cultural heritage.

Earlier in this book, you read about the importance of learning as a shared responsibility. For example, children benefit when they share responsibility for keeping the classroom neat. As children discuss classroom jobs, they can learn the advantages and values of good citizenship as shown in this example.

A teacher began a class discussion saying, "Each day we use this classroom for our work and it gets messy! It is our responsibility to clean it up at the end of each day so that we can easily begin our work the next morning. What do we need to do to clean up our room?"

After children identified the tasks, they proposed jobs such as black-board washer, sweeper, pencil sharpener. On another day they discussed job descriptions and thought about organizing jobs by categories (writing materials, art supplies). They considered how many people were needed to do each task properly, what equipment was needed, and what they would do if someone was absent.

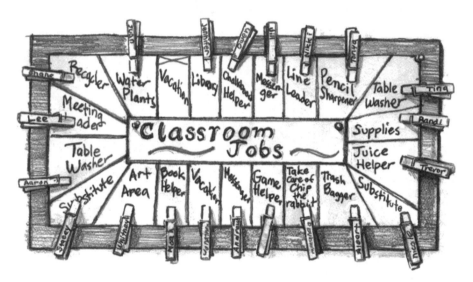

We encourage teachers to recognize how discussions such as this enable children to live the social studies curriculum. The concepts they are learning take on personal meaning as they design systems for the care of their classroom. The teacher creates an environment where children listen to one another and contribute their own ideas. They have to choose jobs and be responsible for getting them done. When there are problems, children become accustomed to bringing issues to the group for consideration and resolution. These experiences in the early grades lay the foundation for children to assume civic responsibility and participate in community affairs as adults. This is reason enough to begin learning social studies in the primary grades.

How Parents Can Help

- Talk about the jobs that each family member does at home: taking out the trash, doing the laundry, setting the table, washing dishes. Make a list together.

- Talk with your children about the work you do either outside the home or in it.

- Talk about your family history. Share family artifacts and look at family photographs. Make a family tree.

- Look at maps to see where relatives were born.

- Teach your children the language of your home culture.

- Explore the city, town, or community where you live. Make a scrapbook of the places you visit together.

- Find out what your child is studying in school. Think about ways you and your child can gather more information about the topic.

- Encourage family discussions about getting along with people. Talk about how you handle disagreements or problems with your friends, and encourage your child to talk about experiences at school.

- Read books and stories about people of different racial, ethnic, religious, and economic backgrounds and about people who lived long ago and in different parts of the world.

- Talk about your beliefs and values and how they influence your thoughts and actions.

Questions to Ask Your Child's Teacher

- What will the class be studying this year? Are there materials or information with which I can help?

- What opportunities will there be for first-hand research?

- What trips will the class be taking?

- How can families become involved?

- What kinds of projects will the children be likely to do related to social studies?

- Can you show me examples of my child's work in social studies?

− 7 −
How Children Become Scientific Thinkers

"Guess what! We're measuring our shadows at school. We have part-ners and we go outside every day at different times and take turns measuring. Then we have to record in our science logs how long they are and write about what we have noticed. My shadow was longer just before we went home today. At lunch time it was really short. I can't wait to see what happens tomorrow."

Scientists "do" science by asking questions, observing carefully, and thinking about the discoveries they make. So, rather than just read-ing in science textbooks about how shadows are formed, children actually need to study their own shadows. Instead of reading about "forms of matter" and drawing or identifying pictures of "different forms of matter," children should construct real experiments using water, ice, and steam and write about their discoveries. To learn sci-ence well, children need opportunities to explore scientific concepts and practice the skills of scientific research as they actively investi-gate answers to questions of interest to them.

What's Involved in Scientific Thinking

At the core of science is the belief that through investigation, one can begin to understand the physical and natural world. Scientists collect data by paying careful attention to detail and making logical and reasonable connections between what they observe and what they know. They ask questions, gather and analyze information, and suggest explanations that can be tested. Children, naturally curious about their world, are eager to explore what they encounter every day—sound, water, light, motion, plants, and animals. Young children want to touch, manipulate, look, and listen in order to create explanations about how the world works. Science instruction should build on this natural enthusiasm.

Using Science Skills

Nurturing children's sense of wonder—their interest and excitement in finding out about the world—is at the heart of learning science. Children can learn science skills as they investigate topics of interest. These skills include:

- asking questions
- making predictions (hypotheses)
- observing with increasing attention to detail
- setting up experiments
- interpreting data and drawing conclusions
- communicating findings

Scientists begin any scientific inquiry by *asking questions*.

Having just listened to the story Owl Moon *by Jane Yolen, a group of children were arguing about whether the moon is out only at night. In response to their enthusiasm, the teacher asked them to suggest ways to find an answer. The children proposed watching the moon for a few days. The teacher suggested they watch for a month. She prepared a recording sheet for them to use and wrote a letter to parents explaining the project.*

This teacher used children's questions to design an experience that would enable them to investigate answers.

By ***making predictions,*** scientists try to anticipate answers to their own questions based on prior knowledge. In school and at home, children can use their own experiences to predict the outcome of situations.

- What do you think will happen when we mix these two paint colors together?

- What would happen if we put this piece of clay into the water?

- What will happen if we wipe the blackboard with a wet sponge? a dry cloth?

Observing with increasing attention to detail means scientists think about what to look for. From each observation experience, children become better observers. Children should be encouraged to use their senses to make observations in many different ways. For example, they can:

- look: discriminate size, color, shape, and position of object; count features; estimate length, volume, or weight.

- touch: determine whether objects feel rough, smooth, wet, dry, oily, scaly, heavy, light, bumpy.

- listen: note the volume or the pitch of sounds.

- smell: describe and identify characteristic odors.

- taste: identify terms such as sweet, bitter, sour, or spicy.

After observing, scientists use the information to make comparisons. They compare their findings about a given object to other known objects so, for example, new sounds or smells are compared to familiar ones, and how and what a particular animal eats is compared to what was observed about another animal.

As children learn to make careful observations, they become familiar with technology and expand their knowledge of tools. With many experiences using different tools–measuring devices, hand lens, microscope, microphone–they will learn how to choose appropriate technology for particular purposes. In addition, if a variety of tools are available and children learn how they can be used, they experience on a daily basis the importance of technology. Tools play an important role in the development of observation as well as other science skills.

Setting up experiments is what scientists do next to test their predictions. Children can learn to plan appropriate experiments and discuss what tools they need to carry them out. In this classroom, a child came up with an erroneous explanation for a scientific phenomenon. This misunderstanding became the basis for lots of experiments.

> *When Peter announced to his teacher that the fish in the tank were drinking the water, she asked him how he knew that. Peter said, "Two reasons. First, they keep opening and closing their mouths. And, second, the water used to be up here," pointing to the water line at the top of the tank, "now it's down to here," pointing to the current water level.*

Peter had observed that the water level in the fish tank gradually diminishes over time. He also saw that the fish were constantly opening and closing their mouths. He came to the mistaken conclusion that the fish were drinking the water. Rather than correcting Peter and teaching the principles of evaporation, his teacher asked him what he thought was happening.

She involved him, along with a group of children, in thinking about and planning experiments to find out what was happening to the water. For example, by observing the water level in another tank without fish, the children saw whether the level stayed the same or changed. They measured the water level over the course of several days and recorded their data. The children did other experiments to observe evaporation, such as washing a chalkboard and painting a fence with water and watching the water evaporate before their eyes. They made chalk lines around puddles after a rain and watched the puddles get smaller and smaller. Peter and the other children concluded that the fish were not drinking the water. The experiments they did also involved them in experiencing the next series of scientific skills.

Scientists *interpret data and draw conclusions*. These skills are central to problem solving and are necessary in many subjects, not just in science. With opportunities to think scientifically, children can observe and experiment, collect information over time, and then carefully analyze what they know. Questions such as these will encourage your child to interpret data and draw conclusions:

- Why is this happening?
- What does the evidence show?
- What do you think happened during the experiment?
- What did we find out?
- What new questions do we have now?

As they answer these types of questions, children will find similarities and differences or organize information into categories. Once children have many experiences organizing information, they begin to relate information from past experiences and apply their knowledge in new ways.

Scientists *communicate their findings* to share and discuss their discoveries. In the classroom, as in real life, reports of scientific findings can take many forms. Sometimes children record their observations for others to see—a one-word caption for first graders or a three-sentence description from third graders. They may make drawings, charts, graphs, and presentations in which they describe what they have done.

Learning Content Through First-Hand Research

First, second, and third graders learn best by actually touching, seeing, hearing, and manipulating the objects or events they are studying—the principle we called active learning in Chapter 1. When science lessons in the classroom are hands-on and children can do first-hand research, they learn best. The location of your child's school automatically suggests a broad range of possible scientific investigations. If a pond or stream is nearby, children can conduct first-hand research about the animals or fish that inhabit it. The construction or demolition of a nearby building, a class pet, or a snowfall can also become the basis for a scientific investigation.

For children to become scientific thinkers, they need to apply science skills to the study of content. The **content** of the science curriculum should blend earth science, life science, and physical science. The following chart illustrates the major content areas and possible topics children in the primary grades might study.

Curriculum Content	**Topics Children Might Investigate**
Living Things (Life science)	*The characteristics, needs, habitats, life cycles, and behavior of birds, fish, insects, plants, or small animals.*
Earth and Space (Earth science)	*Day and night, the moon and stars, seasons, condensation and evaporation, climate and weather, land forms, recycling and garbage, plants and soil.*
Matter (Physical science)	*The properties of substances and how they may be used including structures, building materials, objects that sink and float, liquids and gases.*
Energy (Physical science)	*Light and shadows, mirrors, rainbows, water, ice, and snow, balls and ramps, magnets, electricity, and inventions.*

As in social studies, children learn through in-depth investigations of several content areas during the course of a year.

You can begin to assess the nature of your child's science instruction by asking a few questions. Is your child *mostly* reading about science from a textbook, listening to science stories read aloud, watching videos, or observing demonstrations conducted by a teacher? If the answers are mostly yes, there is a good chance that your child is not involved in active learning experiences and not applying scientific skills. The opportunities to be challenged to think and solve problems are likely to be limited.

However, "hands-on" by itself is not the criterion for good science instruction. Sets of fun science experiments that resemble magic tricks do not indicate a quality program. When science is taught in this manner two problems emerge. First, children miss out on the opportunity to see how the "experiment" fits into a larger body of knowledge. Second, they are less likely to apply what they learn from the experiment to other scientific questions. For example, rather than having children handle and observe worms for twenty minutes, we believe that an in-depth investigation of worms includes many opportunities to observe them, examine pictures, and read books in order to learn about their needs, habitat, life cycle, and behavior. With this type of instruction children learn to organize information, make connections, and see how the specifics of what they are learning relate to the larger natural and physical world. Children also acquire important scientific process skills that they can apply to future learning.

How Science Is Taught

Science instruction shouldn't just happen once a week with a science resource teacher. Children need to study topics that allow them to do extensive research over time. While the science curriculum determines the content to be explored and perhaps, the general topics children might investigate, there should be room to include your child's special interests as well. When children feel they have "chosen" the topic to study, their interests are validated and they are encouraged as learners. If children are collectors and some years (and in some places) they collect worms, or salamanders, or crickets and that's what they talk about, those worms, or salamanders, or crickets are likely to be a promising topic for a scientific study of living things.

The following two examples illustrate how children's interest in a topic can be sustained over time. They also show how children learn science skills as they study particular content. The skills they learn during each investigation can be applied to the next one.

A Study of Living Things

Imagine your child in this first grade class where a study of small creatures is underway. Notice how many science skills they use as they study living things. The children have collected earthworms by searching in piles of decomposing leaves on the playground. At a group meeting, they talked about what they already know and what they would like to know about worms. They decided to try to find out answers to these questions: "Do earthworms have legs?" and "How do earthworms move?"

Children worked with partners using hand lenses to observe the movements of earthworms. They measured their worms with lengths of string. The children looked for clues about how the worms move. They exchanged discoveries about their observations. "My worm is a little rough. When it moves on my hand, it tickles," exclaimed Emily. Teresa said, "I can't seem to measure mine. It gets small and then stretches out very long. It won't stand still." The teacher responded, "Emily, the tickling comes from the bristles on the worm. What do you think those bristles might be for?" And to Teresa she said, "How do you think the worm gets bigger and smaller?" She suggested that the children make large drawings of the worms so that they can display all the parts of the worm that might help the worm to move.

As children continue to do first-hand research, they will come to new understandings of how animals' physical attributes enable them to move or eat and how their habitat contributes to their survival. In the process of studying creatures, children will wonder, question, observe, and pose explanations. They will use scientific thinking skills as they learn about the behavior and characteristics of living things.

A Study of Energy

In working with a teacher we noticed that many children in his class were interested in racing objects (marbles, matchbox cars) and talking about how fast they can ride their bikes. We encouraged him to do a study with balls and ramps as an interesting way for his second graders to learn about energy. Let's look at what children were doing one afternoon:

Small groups of children were constructing tubes, tunnels, and runs for different sized marbles. The teacher challenged the children to build a pathway for the balls that would keep them in motion for as long as possible and cause them to change direction at least once. Children talked about their work as they tested, observed, questioned, and posed explanations. Angie observed, "The higher we start the ball, the farther it goes." Ray asked, "How can we make the ball turn a corner? It keeps going in a straight line." Having tried several balls made of different materials, Tyrone concluded, "The metal ball works better than the glass marble. It bounces less." The teacher asked the children to make drawings of their constructions so that they could share their findings at the class meeting.

In this investigation the children explore important physics concepts: force, gravity, mass, momentum, and friction. Active problem-solving experiences involve them in making decisions about how to conduct an investigation, handle the materials, and effect changes. They talk about what they see and draw conclusions as they work collaboratively.

Making Science Part of Everyday Life in the Classroom

Children need to feel that topics of interest to them are worthy of study. If your child brings objects to school (such as bird nests, insects, and rocks) or shares an experience, these interests can be used by the teacher to encourage scientific explorations as illustrated in this example.

Josie, a first grader, reported during a class meeting on Monday morning that she saw a rainbow over the weekend. Her teacher responded, "Mmm. Let's think about this like scientists. Tell us about what the weather was like when you saw it." After Josie answered, the teacher guided the discussion with other questions including, "What colors did you notice in the rainbow? What happened to the rainbow after the sun went behind a cloud?" A discussion ensued about what causes rainbows.

Daily experiences with objects, plants, animals, and weather provide children with opportunities to think scientifically about the natural and physical world. Interesting materials in the classroom can spark children's thinking. For instance, an invention center might contain boxes of junk (corks, film containers, sponges, spools, balloons, straws, Styrofoam chips, springs, bottle caps, string, cardboard, and wood scraps). Children can be challenged to use these materials to make something that spins, or to invent something that can move objects up and down. A classroom with interesting collections gives children the opportunity to sort and classify objects. And, of course, a tank with fish, hermit crabs, turtles, or a frog or a class pet such as a guinea pig, hamster, or rabbit can be a catalyst for ongoing science discussions and observations.

Your child can learn best by actually being a scientist. In this way he or she will learn scientific skills while exploring topics in life, earth, and physical science.

How Parents Can Help

- Encourage your child to collect and organize objects such as seeds, rocks, marbles, magnets, shells, and bottle caps. Provide a magnifying glass and encourage investigations. You could ask, "What do you notice?" "Which ones do you want to group together?"

- Talk about scientific events that occur in your home: which cereals get soggy, why the food in the back of the refrigerator develops mold, why some plants need to be watered more often than others. Formulate scientific theories with your child about these observations and test them together.

- Show your child that you are interested in science, too. Mix paints, weigh snow, study a rainbow, watch an anthill, predict the weather, and catch fireflies and let them go.

- Sometimes, rather than answering your child's science question, trigger an investigation by asking questions. "Why do you think…?" "What would happen if…?" "How could we find out?"

- Take your child to the library to borrow books and videos on many different science topics.

Questions to Ask Your Child's Teacher

- What science topics will the class be studying this year?

- What opportunities will there be for first-hand research?

- Do you need any materials that I can help you to collect?

- Do you have any trips planned related to science topics?

- How will children record their scientific discoveries?

- What tools do you have available for the children to use for scientific investigations?

- What can I do to help?

– 8 –
How Children's Learning
Is Assessed

"Dad, you know the story I was working on? My teacher said my open-ing paragraph really grabs the reader's attention and she said she couldn't wait to find out what was going to happen. But, you know the part about the accident—she thought it was confusing. Now I have to revise it. I might need your help."

Children are motivated to work hard when they are involved in the assessment process. If they know the teacher's expectations and get specific feedback on their work, children can strive toward a goal. In the example above, the child got appropriate and timely feed-back. As a result, he knows what was good about his writing and what he has to do to improve it.

How does this example compare with your personal experience or your child's experiences with assessment? What are the first words that come to mind when *you* hear the word, **assessment**? Tests? Grades? Report cards? If you are like most parents, you probably hope that the information conveyed by these assessment methods will answer the question, "How is my child doing?" But think about it. Do test scores, grades, and report cards accurately answer the question? Or, should you expect a more detailed, thoughtful, and personal response to your question, "How is my child doing?"

Assessment, as we define it, refers to the tools and processes used to answer specific questions about children's knowledge, skills, behavior, or personality. Assessment of achievement means answering questions about what and how children are learning.

The Purposes of Assessment

Assessment is an important part of your child's education. Information obtained in an accurate and detailed manner can be helpful to everyone involved: parents, children, and teachers. Each purpose serves a different audience.

- Assessment provides information to parents on development and learning.

- Assessment helps children succeed as learners.

- Assessment enables teachers to make changes in instruction.

Assessment Describes Development and Learning

When you receive information about how your child is doing, there are a few big ideas to keep in mind. First, it is helpful to know something about how most children develop. Second, you should hear the whole story.

Knowing about child development will assist you in interpreting assessment information. Remember that six, seven, and eight year old children are not likely to master everything they are taught. Children need time and repeated opportunities to learn certain material before they can internalize it. In addition, young children's growth and learning are not even and do not occur at steady rates. A child's performance generally is not consistent across the board—for example, a good reader may be struggling to form legible letters with a pencil. Thus, in order for you to receive useful information about your child, the teacher must look at all aspects of a child's development.

The "whole story" means getting answers to two different but related questions:

- Has my child made *progress*? In other words, given where he or she began the year, has there been growth?

- How does my child's *performance* compare to expectations for children of the same age or grade level?

If only the first question is answered, you can be left with a misleading impression. For example, you might receive a very positive report about your child's progress at the end of the school year. To your distress and surprise, you attend a conference the following fall and are told that your child is struggling to keep up with the others in the class—in other words, performing below grade level. How did this happen? The end of the year report probably gave information only about your child's *progress*—that there was significant improvement during the year. While this is important information, you also need to know about your child's *performance*—his or her work in comparison to expectations for children in the same grade.

As a parent, you are entitled to a clear and honest description of both your child's progress as measured against his or her own starting point and your child's performance as measured against the standards or expectations for children of the same age and grade level. You also want to know the skills your child has learned and the ones that may need improvement.

Assessment Helps Children Succeed as Learners

Parents are not the only ones who need to know how their children are doing in school. Children also should have this information. You have probably noticed that your child can tell you who is the best runner in the class. Maybe he or she talks about who reads the longest books, writes the best stories, or spells the hardest words. Children this age are deeply invested in what and how everybody else is doing and how they measure up.

But, in many instances, children do not have a clear vision of what "the best" means in terms of their school work or how to achieve it. One all-too-frequent result of leaving children out of the assessment process is a diminished sense of responsibility for their own learning and achievement. In order for you to know if and how your child is involved appropriately in the assessment process, you want to find out if your child:

- knows exactly what is expected of him or her in a given assignment
- gets specific feedback on his or her work
- can describe ways he or she has made progress

Children know what to aim for when expectations are clearly stated. As you read the following anecdote, think about how your child might feel under similar circumstances.

Joshua, a second grader, was especially proud of the story he had written. He felt he had followed the outline the teacher provided. He was quite discouraged, however, when he got his paper back with the comment, "You should recopy this story neatly" written on it.

Joshua's teacher was concentrating on neatness. Joshua's focus and motivation was on the content of the story. Not knowing the teacher's expectations in advance can really discourage a child from even trying to do well. To prevent this outcome, it is necessary to discuss the characteristics of a good project with students at the outset.

When children participate in establishing standards and see models of excellent work, they can better understand what to strive for and how their efforts will be evaluated.

Specific feedback helps children know what they have done well.
Feedback helps a child think about what has been learned, understand how he or she performed in relation to expectations, and provides guidance about what could be done better or where to go next. Without this feedback a child doesn't know how to evaluate work or what to do next to improve. In the next example, Lisa is confused.

> *Lisa, a third grader, completed a research project about rodents after working on it for several weeks. She read two books and recorded several facts about rodents. She traced some pictures from the books and included them in her report. On the date the project was due, she turned it in to the teacher. A week later the report was returned to her with "B" written on it and a sticker of a smiley face. Lisa was confused. Some of her friends got an "A" with their smiley faces. She had no idea why her report was not as good as those of her friends.*

Lisa was puzzled and upset for a reason. She didn't know what she had done well or what could be done better to earn an A.

Evidence of their own progress is important to children. Children compare their work from one time period to another. Because of how children think, they need concrete evidence confirming that they have grown and changed. For example, in January when children look back at math problems they struggled with during the previous fall, six-to-eight-year-olds typically say, "Oh, that is SO easy! I can't believe those problems were so hard for me then!" The practice of collecting work in a portfolio and noting change

over time is a powerful way for children to understand their
own progress.

Assessment Enables Teachers to Modify Instruction

Teachers should be using assessment information to meet the specific
needs of your child. At the beginning of the year, a teacher's instructional plans are based on what children of a particular age can be
expected to know and do. But, because children differ from one
another, and each group of children is unique, these plans must be
modified almost from the first day of school. From your own experience you know that too often children squirm through lessons, bored
because they already know the material. Or, they are confused and
drift off because the material being taught is too difficult for them.

Tailoring instruction to the individual needs of each child benefits all children, including yours. Children should be observed carefully to determine what skills they have and what they are ready to
learn. You can help by letting your child's teacher know about his
or her particular interests, strengths, and special needs. Provide all
the information you can about your child's learning style—how he
or she receives and processes information, participates in activities,
and expresses what has been learned. With information obtained
from careful observations and from discussions with you and your
child, your child's teacher can determine the best instructional plan
for your child.

Effective Approaches to Assessment

Traditionally, assessment came at the end of the learning process.
The teacher conducted a series of lessons on a topic, then gave a
test to find out whether the students learned the required material.
We find that this type of assessment rarely yields information that

can be used to plan instruction, nor does it give students an opportunity to change. Additionally, tests are not considered the most effective way to gather accurate information about students' performance and progress.[24] Current thinking emphasizes assessing what children know and can do, rather than what children do not know. *Performance-based assessment*, a new method of assessment being used throughout the country at all grade levels, means assessing children in real-life settings and in an on-going manner, rather than waiting until the end of a unit of study to give a test.

Valid assessment is not limited to an arbitrary set of skills. Rather, it should give your child an opportunity to demonstrate the full range of his or her knowledge and skills and how your child applies them to real tasks and problems.[25] The work primary grade children do every day—writing stories, making maps, creating paintings, solving math problems—is the best and most logical source of assessment information for both teachers and children. Gathering assessment information from daily activities provides an accurate and complete picture of what children know and can do.

Descriptive Information Is Most Valuable

The more descriptive the information collected in an assessment, the more useful it is to everyone. Report cards with numerical or letter grades alone fail to describe what a child really knows. In addition, many factors can affect what a letter grade means. For example, a child in a high-level reading group might receive a grade of B, while another child, in a lower-level group, might get an A. These two grades have meaning only when the following information is provided:

- an example of the type of reading the child can do (e.g., a page from a reading book)

- an example of the type of reading that children at that particular age or grade level are expected to do

- a description of how the child actually reads (e.g., examples of reading strategies the child uses, specific kinds of errors the child makes)

Descriptive information, whether given as feedback on a child's work or on a report card, means a lot more to children and to parents than a letter or number. This information should first highlight the child's strengths, then describe areas that need improvement, and finally offer recommendations for the child's continued growth. Report cards that you, as parents, receive should explain the teacher's judgments and conclusions.

Children can also have a role in describing their work. When they complete assignments, children can be asked to evaluate their own work. Children might rate their work based on a set of predetermined expectations, or they might simply describe how they feel about their work. Questions such as, "What was easy (difficult) for you?" or "What might you do differently next time?" help children to evaluate their efforts and take increased responsibility for their learning.

A Variety of Methods Are Needed

The tools and approaches used by a teacher to assess your child should be varied as well as descriptive. These can include checklists, descriptions of how children apply skills and knowledge, portfolios of children's work, or logs and journals kept by children themselves.

Checklists. Checklists are lists of skills, usually organized by subject matter, that help teachers to keep track of what children can and can't do. They are often used in formal observations when children do a particular task that allows them to demonstrate skills or knowledge.

Written Observations of Children at Work. How children apply skills and knowledge, approach tasks, relate to others, and make and correct errors, can all be easily and directly observed as they work in the classroom. For instance, as children work collaboratively, they talk about what they are thinking and doing. When they work independently, some children begin writing immediately, while others begin by thinking through a project first. In our experience, we have found that when teachers regularly observe children and keep track of these observations, they note strengths, pinpoint problems, and address them successfully.

Portfolios. Portfolios are collections of children's work. We think that some pieces of work should be chosen by the teacher, and other selections may be chosen by the children themselves. The contents of a portfolio may include a poem, a journal entry, solutions to math problems, a chart from a science experiment, a painting, and a draft and a finished copy of a research report. The purpose of keeping portfolios is to help both children and teachers assess the quality of children's thinking, the effort they put into assignments, and the progress they have made in specific subjects. When children share their portfolios with their parents, you get a real picture of what they can do and their progress over time.

Student Logs. Student logs are records of work done in various subjects. Many effective teachers have children keep records of the books they read, writing the title, author, and a brief summary or comment. Some teachers also have children record science or math investigations, explaining their thinking or procedural steps. We have seen other teachers ask children to keep a daily learning log in

which they record something new they have learned each day. When children document their learning in these ways, they contribute a great deal to the assessment picture.

A variety of assessment methods gives a full picture of how a child approaches tasks, what he or she has learned, and the quality of a child's work compared with expectations for children in his or her grade. In addition, several approaches combined can–and often do–provide a picture of a child's social and physical development as well as intellectual growth.

Conferences Are Part of Assessment

Conferences—between teacher and child, teacher and parent, or teacher, child, and parent—serve to guide instruction and to describe learning. Hence, conferences should be part of the regular classroom routine.

Here are some examples of the kinds of *teacher-child conferences* your child should have with his or her teacher:

- conferences to discuss writing in progress
- conferences where your child reads aloud to the teacher
- conferences to discuss how to solve a math problem
- conferences to get help with an assignment
- conferences to discuss and select work for portfolios

A *parent-teacher conference* is a time for an in-depth exchange of information. To learn the most about your child, think about these things in advance.

- Write down your questions and points you want to make.
- Be prepared to talk about your child and describe your goals.
- Bring examples of any work your child has brought home that you don't understand.

This is what you should expect at the conference.

- The teacher will ask you to talk about your child.
- The teacher will answer any questions you may have about the curriculum.
- If the teacher uses educational jargon that you find confusing, ask for an explanation.

- The teacher will show you examples of your child's work so you can see what your child is learning or to illustrate a point the teacher makes.

- The teacher will give you specific information about your child's strengths and any areas of concern.

- Discuss specific plans for helping your child. Clarify what is expected of your child, the teacher, and you.

Sometimes, *parent-teacher-child conferences* are planned. Many teachers involve children by having them discuss their portfolio work. This can be a very exciting way to observe your child as a student. If parent-teacher-child conferences occur in your child's school, here are some ideas for you to consider.

- Ask your child if he knows about a conference plan.

- Think about whether you have questions or concerns that you wish to raise with the teacher in advance and arrange a time for an additional conference.

What about Conventional Tests

Although conventional tests are frequently used to assess young children's learning, they are more limited than checklists, observation notes, portfolios, and student logs. Why is this the case? There are several reasons.

- Information obtained from conventional tests typically end a unit of study. By this time, it's too late to help a child improve because the unit is finished.

- Conventional tests do not provide a complete picture of what a child knows and can do. For example, a child might spell words correctly on a test, but spell them incorrectly when writing a story.

- Tests do not measure aspects of young children's development that are critical to academic success: self-confidence, the ability to resolve conflicts, or how a child relates to others.

However, conventional tests—both teacher-made and standardized—can be useful assessment tools when they are used in conjunction with other more descriptive types of evaluation. Considered as one method among many, they can ensure a more comprehensive picture of a child's growth and learning.

As a parent, the best way to evaluate assessment practices at your child's school is to think about whether you are getting the information you feel you need about your child.

- Do you have an accurate picture of what your child knows and can do?

- Do you see examples of your child's work and can you observe progress over time?

- Do you have sufficient opportunities to talk with your child's teacher about his progress and performance?

Questions such as these will help you to think about what you know and what more you may need to know.

The Role of National Standards

You may be reading articles in the newspaper or hearing about national standards. In the past few years, leading organizations in various subjects—math, language and literacy, science and technology, social studies, history, geography, the arts, physical education—have developed national standards that define what children should know and be able to do at various grade levels. Content standards refer to the knowledge and skills that should be taught in each discipline. Performance standards refer to the ways to evaluate what children have learned and to judge how well they have learned the knowledge and skills. Many states and school systems are using these standards to develop their own curriculum guidelines.

Standards can provide a useful framework for identifying the important skills and content children should learn and determining how children can demonstrate their learning. There is an important equity issue involved. When standards are agreed upon, everyone knows what to work toward. The process of developing standards has not been easy. Many of the leading teachers and thinkers in the various fields disagree about what should be taught.

While some attempts at defining standards have led to controversy, others, like the math standards (from the National Council of Teachers of Mathematics), which reflect a broad agreement about both content and teaching methods, have had a major impact on math curriculum and instruction. The emphasis on learning to solve problems, which lies at the core of the standards, has transformed the math curriculum in many school districts for the better.

The math standards, in particular, have raised an important related issue. Setting standards is just the first step. Content standards must lead to improved standards of instruction. Teachers have to be given opportunities to assimilate the new content and to learn how to teach in a way that promotes thinking and problem-solving skills. And finally, we have to make sure that children are given the support they need to achieve the standards.

As a nation we must continue the process of developing standards for what and how we teach. Find out what is happening in your school, district, or state.

How Parents Can Help

- Share with your child's teacher what you know about your child's interests, preferred learning styles, and specific needs.

- Talk with your child about the work he or she brings home. Ask questions such as:

  - What do you like best about this?

  - How do you feel you did on this assignment?

  - Would you do something different next time?

  - What was most difficult about this assignment?

  - How did you decide on the topic for this story?

- Model self-evaluation. For example, you might say, "Today was a good day at work. I actually accomplished six of the seven things on my list."

- Give your child specific feedback on projects and chores he or she does around the house. You might say:

  - "You certainly did a careful job cleaning your room. You put everything away."

  - "The Lego building you made is really interesting. I noticed that you spent a long time adding details."

- Acknowledge your child's progress as well as the possibility of further improvement. For example:

  - "Remember when you couldn't swim to the end of the pool? Now you can with no effort!"

  - "It's okay that you weren't able to read all the words on the page. You still figured out the main idea. Nobody learns everything all at once. Keep practicing."

Questions to Ask Your Child's Teacher

- What are my child's strengths and interests in school?

- Are there areas that need strengthening and how can I help my child?

- Can you show me how my child is aware of your expectations on a particular project?

- Can you show me examples of how you give my child feedback related to a particular assignment?

- How often do you conference with children about their work?

- Do you use portfolios to document children's work?

– 9 –
Helping with Homework

"We're starting to study what our town was like a long time ago. We're supposed to interview somebody who's older than fifty about what they remember. Who could I call? And my teacher helped me choose five new spelling words to learn. We picked them out of my journal. I have to practice them by Monday."

When homework is truly work and not a waste of time, children can improve their skills and extend learning beyond school hours. However, homework can also become "homewar," with unpleasant results for everyone. It helps if you know what the teacher's goals are for homework and how and when you should be involved. When parents are involved, they can see what their children are learning, and they can talk with them about what goes on in school.

Homework should reinforce skills and concepts learned at school. Sometimes assignments require children to practice something learned in school or to solve problems. Other assignments may require children to collect information by interviewing a family member or observing objects at home.

For children in first, second, and third grades, homework should also teach responsibility and good work habits. This means helping children learn a system for bringing the assignment home, doing it, and remembering to bring it back to school. You can support your child in this by agreeing on a place where homework will be done, by checking in, as necessary, to make sure the work is in the backpack to go back to school, and finally, that the backpack actually goes to school with your child.

What Is Reasonable

We have found that a reasonable amount of homework in first grade is about ten to fifteen minutes. The assignment might be counting or finding something, asking questions of an adult, or sharing a book. Additional homework time could involve reading with or to family members.

Second and third graders might spend up to thirty minutes on independent homework, which could include spelling words to study, math problems to solve, or math facts to practice. Children may also have projects that involve family members in discussions. In addition they may be expected to spend time reading independently and keeping track of what they read in a log.

What Should You Expect from Your Child's Teacher

Good communication between home and school leads to more positive experiences with homework and prevents "homewar." After many years of teaching and many years of living with our own children's homework assignments, here is what we think you should expect from your child's teacher.

A consistent schedule for homework. Ideally your child's teacher will establish with the children a schedule that shows when assignments will be given and when they will be due. A schedule helps children and families plan ahead so everyone knows, for example, that spelling words come home one day and math another. If your child does not seem to have a homework schedule, you might mention to the teacher how helpful it would be for you.

Clear directions and expectations. It's important for your child to know what is expected in homework assignments. For example, in a writing assignment, are all the words to be spelled correctly? Should you correct them? If your child doesn't know what to do, you should send a note to the teacher explaining the difficulty.

A method for transporting homework. It's not unusual for homework to be crumpled and torn because it was stuffed in a backpack or pocket. If your child's teacher has not provided a special folder for transporting homework, you may want to consider what your child needs to get his or her homework back and forth from school neatly.

A variety of homework assignments. Homework assignments should vary. Assignments can include a mix of some practice exercises (math facts, spelling words) as well as some interesting work that involves talking with or interviewing people, finding out information around the house (looking for patterns, counting windows, measuring a room), and reading together.

How Parents Can Help

- Establish a place in the house where your child can do homework. Most first and second graders are not yet able to go to their rooms or to do their homework in a place where they are alone.

- Make sure the materials your child will need are available, such as pencils, markers, crayons, paper, scissors, and ruler.

- Identify the best time for your child to do homework. Some children need a break when they come home before beginning to work; others like to do what they can immediately. Most parents find that it is best not to leave homework (other than reading) to do just before bedtime. Six-to-eight year olds are just too tired by then.

- If necessary, post a schedule that shows when homework is due and when your child will do it each day.

- Decide with your child about rules, such as "no TV during homework time."

- Monitor how much time your child spends on homework. (This doesn't include getting a snack, bouncing balls, or running around the room!) If your child is spending more than a reasonable time on homework each day, talk with the teacher.

Questions to Ask Your Child's Teacher

- What are your expectations for how much time my child should spend on different kinds of homework?

- How do your homework assignments extend what children are doing in the classroom?

- How is homework reviewed in school? Do you review it or is there a peer review system?

- Is my child handing in homework on time and properly completed?

- How can I further help my child at home?

Conclusion

"The elementary grades constitute a defining experience for children—one that will heavily influence the life course from middle childhood to adolescence and beyond. The importance of success in school is profound. A child's fundamental sense of worth as a person depends substantially on the ability to achieve in school." [26]

We hope this statement from the Carnegie Task Force on Learning in the Primary Grades confirms what you have been thinking. It supports our belief in the importance of these early grades of elementary school. The Task Force's recent report examines the developmental and learning needs of children aged three to ten in this country. The Report highlights the importance of high quality elementary school experiences for children and describes best practices based on their research.

Years of Promise: A Comprehensive Learning Strategy for America's Children states that schools fail our children for many reasons, including "the heavy reliance of schools on outmoded or ineffective curricula and teaching methods."[27] This book offers an alternative by showing what effective learning looks like. Our schools are not predestined to fail. Schools can be places where children are happy, where they learn and thrive. Your child should have these kinds of experiences in school.

We have described effective curricula and teaching methods that work for all children. Good teaching practices cross economic, racial, cultural, and other differences because they are designed to meet the needs of individual children in the classroom. We have seen such classrooms where children are eager to learn and classrooms that encourage, rather than inhibit, learning.

You now have a picture of what learning can be like in first, second, and third grade classrooms with curricula that responds to how children learn best. The stories we have told of real teachers and real children show what day-to-day learning and instruction can look like.

We have offered you a way to look at what is happening in your child's classroom and assess whether it meets your child's needs. If what is happening in your child's classroom reflects the approaches you read about in this book, you now have some additional ideas about how to work effectively with an excellent teacher to extend your child's learning. If your child's classroom does not resemble any of the models presented here, we encourage you to use this book as a guide to expand your own role as your child's advocate. We hope our book will help you to work with other parents, teachers, principals, and school boards to help bring about the changes you desire. The more you know about excellent classrooms, the more effectively you can support both your child and his or her teachers.

Glossary

Child-centered or child-initiated learning focuses on giving children opportunities to explore and make discoveries through planned experiences related to the subjects under study. The phrase is used as a contrast to other learning experiences which are more teacher directed. (See "teacher directed learning" below.)

Collaborative or cooperative learning describes a process in which children work together on particular projects with specific academic and social goals in mind. The term is also used to describe an environment in the classroom that encourages children to help each other learn by sharing information and ideas.

Conflict resolution refers to a systematic process for dealing peacefully with disagreements. Some schools offer specific training to everyone in the school community to promote a consistent approach.

Constructing knowledge describes a belief that children learn by applying new information to what they already know in order to interpret what they observe and make sense of the new experience. They build new and deeper understandings about the world through a process of testing out ideas, and acquiring and refining skills. To enable children to construct knowledge, learning builds from what children know and can experience first hand.

Critical thinking is a phrase used to describe an important educational goal. Critical thinkers can apply their knowledge and skills to analyze and solve problems, address questions, and seek additional information.

Developmentally appropriate practice describes a philosophical framework based on a set of beliefs about teaching and learning. Teachers in schools and classrooms that describe themselves as developmentally appropriate make decisions about children's education based on a knowledge of child development—how children grow and develop emotionally, socially, cognitively, and physically; a knowledge of the individual characteristics of the children in a class—their strengths, interests, and needs; and a knowledge of the cultural context in which children have been raised.

Emotional intelligence refers to a set of characteristics—motivation, persistence, impulse and mood control, empathy, and hope—as contrasted with academic intelligence. New research about how the brain works concludes that social competence may be even more important than I.Q. to success in life. Many believe that children can learn emotional intelligence if classrooms and teachers teach particular skills and that increased competence in this area aids intellectual ability.

Hands-on learning describes the kinds of experiences children are engaged in as they learn. Hands-on learning typically involves active experiences using materials, manipulating objects, doing experiments, interviewing people, reading, writing, and talking, rather than more passive learning experiences during which children sit and listen to the teacher or instructor.

Invented spelling describes a process in which children spell words the way the words sound to them, thus "inventing" spelling. Invented spelling is encouraged by teachers so that children can do substantial amounts of writing before many have a command of the standard spelling of the English language. Children are asked to think about and use their growing knowledge of phonics as a tool to write. As children progress as writers, they will be expected to learn standard or conventional spelling and to edit their writing accordingly.

Multiple intelligences refers to the work of the psychologist Howard Gardner who expanded the concept of intelligence by analyzing the different ways children are smart. He has identified seven different kinds of intelligence: logical-mathematical, linguistic, musical, spatial, bodily kinesthetic, interpersonal, and intrapersonal. The result of his research has been to spur schools and teachers to consider the many ways people acquire information and skills and to expand the opportunities we offer children to demonstrate their learning.

Phonics refers to a reading strategy taught to beginning readers to help them to pronounce words by learning the sounds made by individual letters and groups of letters. Critics contend however, that because the English language has more exceptions than rules related to sounds, this strategy by itself is inadequate. Some proponents promote phonics as the primary method of teaching children to read—a phonics first, or phonics only approach. Research clearly indicates that instruction in letter sounds and patterns should be part of a balanced approach to teaching children to read.

Problem-solving skills is a phrase used to explain that children need to use the skills and knowledge they learn in ways that make sense. In other words, it is not enough to know how to add and subtract large numbers but to know when to apply this knowledge in a real situation. Problem-solving skills are not taught in isolation from particular content, but as part of the hands-on, active experiences teachers use to guide instruction.

Teacher directed learning is a term used to contrast with student or child-centered learning. While many classroom experiences are teacher directed, this phrase refers to a style of teaching in which most information is "told" to students rather than child-centered or student-initiated learning, where children have more opportunities to explore and discover and the teacher's role is that of a facilitator, coach, or guide.

Whole language refers to a set of beliefs about how children acquire language skills. Because internal motivation is considered key to language and literacy development, proponents advocate that children have many positive experiences reading and writing without necessarily learning specific skills as a precondition. Whole language is based on the understanding that reading is about finding meaning and that many children learn to recognize words and phrases in context. Skills in phonics as well as other reading strategies are taught as part of many interesting reading and writing activities.

Writing or writer's workshop is a special writing time used in many classrooms to capture children's interest and excitement about being authors and doing what "real" writers do. During regularly scheduled writing times, children make choices about what to write about and, as they progress, spend substantial time revising and editing their work. They are taught specific skills as part of this process.

Developmental Characteristics of 1st, 2nd, and 3rd Graders

Six to eight year olds have their own particular characteristics. You may have noticed that your child, for example, has begun to define him or herself based on certain attributes or achievements, such as: "I wear glasses." "I'm good at soccer." "I can read books with chapters." Children this age are defining who they are based on certain simple attributes. Many think about how they look in the eyes of others and become increasingly self-conscious. Establishing friendships becomes very important for most children this age, although they sometimes lack the skills necessary to do so. A delightful characteristic of this age is the emergence of a sense of humor—telling jokes can be a favorite pastime. Children this age also become less dependent on adults and more dependent on peers. As this occurs, children may begin to question authority, yours and others, and test limits.

Think about your child and his or her playmates of the same age. Some are taller or shorter, some seem more or less coordinated. One child may be very verbal with a large vocabulary while another says little. While there are predictable patterns of development, children do not grow and develop at the same rate. A good rule to remember in thinking about child development is that in any group of children the same age there is likely to be a two-and-a-half year span of development. In addition, an individual child's development does not follow an even course across all areas: a six year old may have the fine motor skills of some seven year olds but the language skills of some five year olds.

The Transition from Five to Six

Five year olds revel in their newly acquired skills. They are generally full of joy and it is a great time for parents and other important adults in their lives because children this age want to please and show affection. At the same time, fives are very focused on themselves. They learn by doing things themselves rather than by watching or listening to instructions. Sharing can be frustrating as can trying to understand another person's point of view. Fantasy play is a favorite pastime and fantasy and reality are sometimes confused in their minds.

While they may sound like adults because they use language with ease, fives need lots of adult support and guidance to negotiate with friends and make transitions from one activity to another. Most five year olds do not yet have the ability to use their eyes efficiently or easily to scan a page from left to right. That's why formal reading instruction should wait. Since fives are usually calmer than they were at four, many parents expect to get lots of information about school and other activities. But, that is not the way of fives. The most effective way to find out more is to get involved in their make-believe play with animals, puppets, trucks, stuffed animals or dolls. As children turn six, they often move into a less stable phase, becoming more moody.

Six Year Olds

If you are the parent of a six year old, you may remember last year as "the good old days." Six year olds can be amazingly moody! One minute they are friendly and enthusiastic, and the next, they are rebellious and irritable. Their best friend becomes their worst enemy within a matter of seconds, only to be their best friend again. Tears and tantrums, laughter and silliness are all common expressions.

While six year olds want to make friends, they may be very bossy and not understand why they are sometimes rebuffed. They can be very competitive and being first (or last) and winning are important. Many six year olds also don't take criticism well.

As learners, most six year olds are very curious. They learn best through their active involvement with people and materials. The product is usually less important to them than the process of getting there. For many, their thinking is beginning to change: they can now recognize that two sets of ten objects are equivalent even when one is spread apart and the other is clustered together.

Physically, many six year olds can seem to be in perpetual motion; they squirm as they sit, or gesture with their bodies as they talk. They love to run and jump, throw and catch, do cartwheels and somersaults, and are gradually gaining control of fine motor activities as well, using pencils, scissors, brushes, and markers with increasing ease.

Seven Year Olds

Seven year olds can be highly self-critical children who worry about making mistakes. Many children this age are eager to master new skills and begin to demand perfection of themselves. Some children draw the same picture or write stories about the very same theme over and over, striving to achieve perfection. They take life seriously and often feel that things are unjust. Schedules and routines are important to them and they want them followed exactly.

Fortunately, this same perfectionist is evolving into a more capable social being. They can work with others more successfully and listen to and appreciate the contributions of others. Some seven year olds also, however, want time to work alone. Many develop special interests such as collecting baseball cards, doing gymnastics, playing a musical instrument, or playing soccer. Their tendency toward repetitive actions can be seen in their desire to play the same game over and over.

Like six year olds, sevens continue to learn most readily through concrete experiences and active participation. They enjoy experimenting and have the intellectual capacity to organize their experiences mentally. Most seven year olds are willing to take time to think and plan before they set out to work. Many enjoy imaginative play and like to put on puppet shows and dramatize stories.

Seven year olds have increased stamina, control, and balance and a greater interest in team sports. Like the six year old, most sevens are active and energetic and sometimes unable to control their energy. Their increased and improved eye-hand coordination enable them to draw and write more easily, although copying from the blackboard is still difficult.

Eight Year Olds

At eight, even the most delightful child can be very argumentative. Children of this age gradually begin to view themselves as individuals in the context of the larger world and they are keenly aware of the difference between the adult world and their own. Frustrated with limitations, they want to assert themselves. They can argue a point forever!

Friendships continue to be very important to most eights even though they have endless disagreements. Eight year olds like to form clubs and spend time planning who will be included and who will be excluded. Many like team games and group projects and discussions. Traditions become very important to them and special roles are prized.

Eight year olds have the capacity for more abstract thinking as long as what they are thinking about relates to something they have experienced directly. As they begin to study historical information and learn about the experiences of people long ago, they make comparisons to their own experiences. Although they continue to learn best through active, concrete experiences, they can use books as a source of information as well. By age eight, most children have a longer attention span. They are usually able to think and reason logically, and enjoy collecting, organizing, and classifying objects and information. Imaginative play in the form of skits, role plays, and puppet shows continues to be an important learning tool for many eight year olds.

Parents of eight year olds know about high energy. Many children this age enjoy rough and tumble play such as tackling games, as well as games that call for exactness, such as team sports (soccer or softball). They take pleasure in the physical skills they have acquired and may be physically daring. Their fine muscle work shows increased speed and smoothness. This is also the age when some children write with tiny letters and their artwork becomes smaller and more detailed.

Becoming Nine

As children turn nine we often see predictable changes. They love to be praised for their efforts. At the same time, they want to be recognized as an independent person and as strongly aligned with their peer group. Nines need and want an adult to talk things over with. Nines begin to see things from a variety of perspectives and with their longer attention spans and increased ability to think abstractly, they can take on learning projects less tied to the here and now. They are ready for the new responsibilities and expectations of fourth grade.

Learning Disabilities, Special Needs, and Inclusion

As a parent, you want to be sure your child is getting the attention he or she needs to succeed in school. If you are concerned that your child may be having trouble learning or is doing well in some areas and in others seems too far behind, and you're puzzled about why, you should seek information and guidance. The early grades of school are an important time to give children the help they need. Talk first with your child's teacher and find out if the teacher also sees what you see. Ask about evaluations that can be done at school to gather more information. If you are still uneasy, you may want to do some research. Read about learning disabilities, contact organizations that can give you information about services and testing, and/or seek professional help on your own.

If you have a child with diagnosed disabilities, you need specific information about your entitlements under federal law. If your child's classroom includes children with significant disabilities who require special attention, you may have concerns about whether and how the teacher is able to accommodate special-needs children along with your own.

Any response to these concerns is not simple and depends on many variables. While a child with a disability often requires specialized support, a classroom atmosphere that emphasizes a respect for differences and values each person's ability to make a contribution can work well for all children if appropriate support services are available.

Under the Individuals with Disabilities Education Act of 1990 (IDEA)[28], all children have a legal right to a free, appropriate public education in the least restrictive environment. This means that in more and more schools across the country, children with significant disabilities are now included in regular classrooms. The disabilities range from autism, hearing and visual problems, physical disabilities requiring wheelchairs or prosthetic devices, and learning disabilities of many kinds. Whereas in the past the norm was to serve children in specialized schools or in special classrooms, today the pendulum has swung toward inclusion programs. The law provides for parents, teachers, and special education experts to work together to determine what is best for the child. They must also consider the additional burdens on the school district. Each child and each situation is unique and has to be determined individually.

What are the results of including children with disabilities in a regular classroom? For children with special-needs, research shows that they do better academically and socially than when they are served in separate settings.[29] Research also indicates that benefits for other children may include learning tolerance, gaining a better understanding of the needs of others, and learning to feel comfortable being around people different from themselves.[30] As parents, however, you should understand that for inclusion to work well for all children, teachers need additional classroom support and the advice of experts.

Making Inclusion Work for The Child with a Disability

As the parent of a child with a disability in a mainstream classroom, you want to do everything you can to help your child succeed. It is essential that you seek the advice and support of a parent advocacy group in your area to make sure that you have the information you need to obtain the best services for your child. For example, every child who is classified as having a disability must receive an individualized education program or IEP, which describes what the particular learning goals are for your child and how the school will meet them. Parents are encouraged to work with school personnel to develop and review their child's IEP annually.

Parent groups can also keep you up to date on changes in federal legislation. Congress is expected to modify the IDEA in 1997. Some provisions likely to change are of particular interest to parents of a child with disabilities. Whereas current legislation focuses on categories of disabilities, the revised legislation may encourage more of a focus on individual needs across categories. Another change may affect the numbers of children served.

Up to now states defined the children eligible for services and received funding based on the number of children identified. It is likely that the new legislation will provide funds to states using a formula based on population and poverty statistics. This means that states and school districts may have less incentive to identify and serve large numbers of children because the number served will not affect the funding they receive. Parents and teachers may need to be more resourceful in pursuing requests for services for children who they think meet the special needs requirements.

Parent support groups and advocacy organizations can also guide you in ways to help the teachers working with your child and provide suggestions about communicating information about your child to his or her classmates and their parents. Enlisting the support of other parents of children in the class can go a long way toward making inclusion a positive experience for everyone.

Making Inclusion Work for the Non-Disabled Child

If your child is in a classroom with a child or children with disabilities, you may want to find out more about the support services available to assist the teacher. For example, if the child with a disability receives assistance from another adult in the classroom, all children are likely to benefit from having an additional adult around. On the other hand, if such support is not available, all children can suffer.

While recognizing a family's right to privacy, you may want to encourage the family of the child with a disability to talk with you, other parents, and the children in the class about their child's strengths as well as the nature of the disability. With the parents' involvement, you can learn what the school and the teacher are doing to support the child and what you and your child can do to help.

As we mentioned, Congress is likely to make changes in the IDEA legislation in 1997. To learn about how these changes may affect your child, contact the organizations that follow. As the educational community learns more about meeting the needs of different kinds of learners, all children are offered more variety in the ways they are taught and in the ways they can demonstrate their learning.

The following organizations can give you more information about these and other related issues.

National Parent Network on Disabilities
1727 King Street, Suite 305
Alexandria, VA 22314

(703)684-6763

National Information Center for Children & Youth with Disabilities
P.O. Box 1492
Washington, DC 20013

(800)695-0285
nichy@acd.org

ERIC Clearinghouse on Disabilities & Gifted Education
Council for Exceptional Children
1920 Association Drive
Reston, VA 20191-1589

(800)328-0272
ericec@cec.sped.org

Office of Special Education & Rehabilitation Services
US Department of Education
330 C St., SW
Switzer Bldg., Room 3132
Washington, DC 20202-2524

(202)205-8241

Resources

Child Development

Beyond Discipline: From Compliance to Community, Alfie Kohn, Alexandria, VA: Association for Supervision and Curriculum Development, 1996. (1-800-933-2723) This book challenges most assumptions about discipline in the classroom. He suggests that parents and teachers have to think beyond control with its focus on behavior, rules, and compliance, and consider how to involve children as creative problem solvers who take responsibility for making decisions that improve their community. Self-disciplined children, according to studies reported by Kohn, who are decision makers at school, are more self-confident and interested learners.

Continuing on Track...As Your Child Grows & Learns, Colorado Department of Education, 1996. (FAX 303-830-0793) This brochure, developed by the Early Childhood Initiatives team, gives brief descriptions of what most 5, 6, 7, and 8 year olds are like and suggestions for activities parents can do with their child and ways to respond constructively to problems.

Emotional Intelligence, Daniel Goleman, New York: Bantam Books, 1995. Goleman demonstrates how important it is to nurture children's development so that they become emotionally intelligent, that is, they show self-awareness, impulse control, persistence, self-motivation, empathy, and social deftness. He argues that high I.Q. alone doesn't guarantee a person's success in life. Instead, emotional intelligence is a better predictor. He shows how we need these skills to better our personal relationships and to perform in a workforce that requires teamwork and cooperation. Goleman concludes with information about how parents and school programs can teach these skills.

The Learning Child, Guidelines for Parents & Teachers, Dorothy Cohen, New York: Pantheon Books, 1971. With joy and humor Dr. Cohen describes child development in the years from five to eleven and describes what and how much children can learn during these years. This book is written for parents to provide glimpses of children's lives at school. It remains, after more than twenty-five years, a relevant and informative book.

Playground Politics, Understanding the Emotional Life of Your School-Age Child, Stanley I. Greenspan, M.D. with Jacqueline Salmon, Reading, MA: Addison-Wesley Publishing Company, 1993. Using the stories of real children, Dr. Greenspan captures how children grow and develop socially and emotionally during the years five to twelve and helps parents see and understand how to support their child during these years.

Schools, Families, and School Reform

At Home in Our Schools, A Guide to Schoolwide Activities that Build Community, Ideas from the Child Development Project for Parents, Teachers and Administrators, Oakland, CA: Developmental Studies Center, 1994. (1-800-666-7270) The Child Development Project has worked over the past decade to demonstrate through research and practice that schools that create "caring communities" can teach prosocial values and have a challenging, relevant curriculum. This book shows how a variety of schoolwide activities (science fairs, movie nights, family reading projects) can support values such as inclusion and participation, cooperation, appreciation of differences, helping others, and taking responsibility.

MegaSkills® How Families Can Help Children Succeed in School and Beyond, Dorothy Rich, Boston: Houghton Mifflin Company, 1988 and *MegaSkills®: In School and Life—The Best Gift You Can Give Your Child*, Dorothy Rich, Boston: Houghton Mifflin Company, 1992. These books for parents describe how to help children acquire the skills they need to be life-long learners, who go beyond the basics because they have confidence, motivation, initiative, and perseverance, just a few of the "megaskills" she describes. With thoughtful attention to the needs of toddlers to 12 year olds, Dr. Rich suggests hundreds of carefully designed activities parents can do with children and strategies to encourage children to learn to work hard, use good judgment, and show concern for others. In fall, 1997, Dr. Rich will have a new book: *What Do We Say? What Do We Do? Parents and Children Solve Home-School Problems Together* (Tor).

A Parent's Guide to Innovative Education - Working with Teachers, Schools, and Your Children for Real Learning, Anne Wescott Dodd, Chicago: The Noble Press, Inc. 1992. (312-642-1168) In this book, a teacher writes about new ways of thinking about education and why "the good old days" really weren't so good after all. She talks about the changes that must come at the classroom level and urges parents to become advocates for their children.

Reaching Potentials: Transforming Early Childhood Curriculum and Assessment, Vol. II, Sue Bredekamp and Teresa Rosegrant, Editors, Washington, DC: National Association for the Education of Young Children, 1995. (1-800-424-2460) This is a book for educators that parents can use to get a sense of the content of curriculum across the age span 3–8 and how teachers think about the process of teaching content and skills.

Curriculum Content

Children's Software Revue, Warren Buckleitner, Editor, 44 Main Street, Flemington, NJ 08822. (1-800-993-9499) This newsletter, published six times a year, reviews educational software for children ages 3-to-14. Reviewers include children and families, teachers, and staff. There are excellent descriptions of the strengths and weaknesses of a given title plus system requirements. Also included are articles about the appropriate use of computers and software. This will really help parents make decisions about what to buy.

Constructing Curriculum for the Primary Grades, Diane Trister Dodge, Judy R. Jablon, and Toni S. Bickart, Washington, DC: Teaching Strategies, Inc., 1994. (1-800-637-3652) This book guides teachers in integrating the best practices in classroom management and curriculum content for grades 1-3. It defines six strategies that provide a framework for making decisions and implementing curriculum. These strategies emphasize creating a learning environment where children learn skills and knowledge and respect and responsibility. Teachers use these strategies to address language and literacy, mathematical and scientific thinking, social studies, and the arts and technology.

Exploring Everyday Math, Ideas for Students, Teachers, and Parents, Maja Apelman and Julie King, Portsmouth, New Hampshire: Heinemann, 1991. (1-800-541-2086) This book describes activities which begin at school and continue at home. Parents and children work together to investigate and solve problems.

Families Writing, Peter R. Stillman, Portsmouth, New Hampshire: Heinemann, 1989. (1-800-541-2086) If you are interested in ideas for writing projects as a family, this book will help. In addition there is information about methods of writing and suggestions for encouraging readers.

Invitations, Changing as Teachers and Learners K-12, Regie Routman, Portsmouth, New Hampshire: Heinemann, 1991. (1-800-541-2086) This is a book for teachers that describes in detail what a whole language approach is all about and the particular strategies teachers use to teach reading and writing. The back of the book, called *The Blue Pages: Resources for Teachers from Invitations*, is offered as a stand-alone volume. It provides an extensive annotated list of books for children organized by grade level.

Raising a Reader, Make Your Child a Reader for Life, Paul Kropp, New York: Doubleday, 1996. This book is all about what you can do as a parent to help your child learn to read and enjoy reading. You will find information about excellent instruction, what to look for in your child's school, how to choose books with your child, and ideas for family reading activities.

Science for All Americans, Scientific Literacy: What is it? Why America needs it. How we can achieve it. F. James Rutherford and Andrew Ahlgren, New York: Oxford University Press, 1990. The authors, both involved in the development of national science standards, explain what scientific literacy is needed for the next century. They urge schools not to teach more content, but to focus on key concepts and principles and teach them more effectively.

Learning Disabilities, Special Needs, and Inclusion

Exceptional Parent Magazine, PO Box 3000, Dept. EP, Denville, NJ 07834. (1-800-247-8080) Now in its 26th year of publication, *Exceptional Parent* magazine is an excellent resource for parents of children and young adults with disabilities and special health care needs. The September 1996 issue includes a well-rounded debate on the inclusion issue by parents of special needs children.

Keys to Parenting a Child with a Learning Disability, Barry E. McNamara, , Francine J. McNamara. New York: Barron's Educational Series, 1995. The authors provide a practical course of action for parents who suspect a learning disability in their child. They also describe methods of special education, dealing with learning disabled children at home, and integrating them into community activities.

Negotiating the Special Education Maze, A Guide for Parents and Teachers, Third Edition, Winifred Anderson, Stephen Chitwood, and Deidre Hayden. Bethesda, MD: Woodbine House, 1997. (1-800-843-7323) Recognizing that parents are the best advocates for their child, this book walks parents through the process of getting help for their child as mandated by the Individuals with Disabilities Education Act (IDEA). It is one of the best resources available to parents for understanding the early intervention and special education systems.

No Easy Answers: The Learning Disabled Child at Home and at School, Sally L. Smith,New York: Bantam Doubleday Dell Publishing Group, Inc., 1995. This book gives parents the information they need to understand what is going on with their learning disabled child. The book has chapters on different disabilities and includes information on legislation that guarantees an equal education for learning disabled children. There is also information on learning disabled adults.

National Standards

Benchmarks for Science Literacy, Project 2061. American Association for the Advancement of Science. New York: Oxford University Press, 1993.

Curriculum and Evaluation Standards for School Mathematics, National Council of Teachers of Mathematics, 1989. (1-800-235-7566)

Curriculum Standards for Social Studies, Expectations of Excellence. National Council for the Social Studies, 1994. (3501 Newark St. N.W., Washington, DC 20016)

Geography for Life, National Geography Standards. Geography Education Standards Project, 1994.

Moving Into the Future, National Standards for Physical Education, A Guide to Content and Assessment. National Association for Sport and Physical Education, 1995.

National Science Education Standards. National Academy of Sciences, National Academy Press, 1996. (1-800-624-6242)

National Standards for Civics and Government (Draft, November, 1994). Center of Civic Education Calabasas, CA. (818-591-9321)

Performance Standards, Vol. 1 Elementary School, English Language Arts, Mathematics, Science, Applied Learning, New Standards. National Center on Education and the Economy and the University of Pittsburgh, 1997. (202-783-3668)

Standards for the English Language Arts. A Project of the International Reading Association and National Council of Teachers of English, 1996. (1-800-336-READ, ext. 266)

World Wide Web Sites

Here is a brief listing of some World Wide Web sites that deal with parenting and education issues. This list is by no means exhaustive and new sites pop up every day. Many of these sites include extensive links to other related areas. Start here and have fun exploring—you'll find statistics, articles, resources, organizations, activities you can do with your children, books, and a lot more!

Parent Involvement

Alliance for Parental Involvement (ALLPIE)	http://www.croton.com/allpie
Families and Education	http://www.famed.org
Family.com	http://www.family.com
Family Education Network	http://familyeducation.com
Family Involvement in Education (U.S. Department of Education)	http://www.ed.gov/Family
Family Planet	http://familyweb.starwave.com
Kidsource	http://www.kidsource.com
National Parent Information Network	http://ericps.ed.uiuc.edu/npin/npinhome.html
National PTA	http://www.pta.org/pta/defaultsamp.asp
Parent Soup	http://www.parentsoup.com
Project Appleseed	http://members.aol.com/pledgenow/appleseed/index.html

Children's Literature and Software

Children's Literature Web Guide	http://www.ucalgary.ca/~dkbrown/index.html
Gryphon House	http://www.ghbooks.com
Superkids Educational Software Review	http://www.superkids.com

Education Links, Advocacy, News, Statistics

Charter Schools	http://coled.umn.edu/charter.html
Children Now	http://www.childrennow.org
The Daily Report Card	http://yn.la.ca.us/drc/drc.html
Developing Educational Standards	http://putwest.boces.org/Standards.html
ERIC Clearinghouse on Elementary and Early Childhood Education	http://cricps.ed.uiuc.edu/ericeece.html
List of Internet Sites for Schools, School Districts and State Boards of Education	http://rrnet.com/~gleason/k12.html
National Center for Education Statistics	http://www.ed.gov/NCES/pubs/D95
Profiles of Every School District in the Country	http://www.sunspace.com

Special Needs

ERIC Clearinghouse on Disabilities and Gifted Education	http://www.cec.sped.org/ericcec.htm
Family Village	http://www.familyvillage.wisc.edu
National Association for Gifted Children	http://www.nagc.org
National Parent Network on Disabilities	http://www.npnd.org

Endnotes

1. Diane Trister Dodge, Judy R. Jablon, and Toni S. Bickart, *Constructing Curriculum for the Primary Grades* (Washington, DC: Teaching Strategies, Inc., 1994).

2. Erik Erikson, *Childhood and Society* (New York: W.W. Norton & Co., 1963).

3. Stanley Greenspan, *Playground Politics: Understanding the Emotional Life of Your School-Age Child* (New York: Addison-Wesley Publishing Co., 1993), 9.

4. James B. Greeno and Rogers P. Hall, "Practicing Representation, Learning with and About Representational Forms," *Phi Delta Kappan* 78:5 (1997): 361–67.

5. Elliot W. Eisner, "Cognition and Representation: A Way to Pursue the American Dream?" *Phi Delta Kappan* 78:5 (1997): 349–53.

6. B. McCombs, "Processes and Skills Underlying Intrinsic Motivation to Learn: Toward a Definition of Motivational Skills Training Intervention." *Educational Psychologist* 19 (1984): 197–218; and D. Schunk, "Goal Setting and

Self-Efficiency During Self-Regulated Learning." *Educational Psychologist* 25:1 (1990): 71–86.

7. Renate Caine, *Making Connections: Teaching and the Human Brain* (Alexandria, VA: ASCD, 1991); and Sylvester, Robert, *A Celebration of Neurons: An Educator's Guide to the Human Brain* (Alexandria, VA: ASCD, 1995).

8. R. Kotulak, "Brain Development in Young Children: New Frontiers for Research, Policy and Practice," keynote address to Carnegie Task Force on Learning in the Primary Grades, 13 June 1996.

9. Howard Gardner, *Multiple Intelligences: The Theory in Practice* (New York: Basic Books, 1993).

10. Daniel Goleman, *Emotional Intelligence* (New York: Bantam Books, 1995).

11. Anne T. Henderson, ed., *The Evidence Continues to Grow: Parent Involvement Improves Student Achievement* (Washington, DC: National Committee for Citizens in Education, 1987).

12. Daniel Goleman, *Emotional Intelligence* (New York: Bantam Books, 1995), 27.

13. R.E. Slavin, *Cooperative Learning* (New York: Longman, 1983); and N. Davidson and T. Worsham, eds., *Enhancing Thinking Through Cooperative Learning* (New York: Teachers College Press, 1992).

14. For further discussion of phonics, see Regie Routman, *Literacy at the Crossroads* (Portsmouth, NH: Heinemann, 1996).

15. Eric A. Kimmel, *The Gingerbread Man Retold* (New York: Holiday House, 1993).

16. *Years of Promise: A Comprehensive Learning Strategy for America's Children*, report of the Carnegie Task Force on Learning in the Primary Grades (New York: Carnegie Corporation, September, 1996), 104–7.

17. Regie Routman, *Invitations: Changing as Teachers and Learners K–12* (Portsmouth, NH: Heinemann, 1994).

18. L.K. Clarke, "Invented Versus Traditional Spelling in First Graders' Writings: Effects on Learning to Spell and Read," *Research in the Teaching of English* 22 (1988): 281–309.

19. Lucy McCormick Calkins, *The Art of Teaching Writing*, New Edition (Portsmouth, NH: Heinemann, 1994).

20. *Curriculum and Evaluation Standards for School Mathematics* (Reston, Virginia: National Council of Teachers of Mathematics, Inc., 1989).

21. Cuisenaire rods and unifix cubes are colorful materials children use to construct numbers and solve problems.

22. a journal used to record math activities

23. paper with a picture of a geoboard on it

24. J. Herman and S. Golan, "The Effects of Standardized Testing on Teaching and Schools," *Educational Measurement: Issues and Practice* 20:42 (1993); and R. Calfee and E. Hiebert, "The Teacher's Role in Using Assessment to Improve Learning," *Assessment in the Service of Learning: Proceedings of the 1987 ETS Invitational Conference* (Princeton, NJ: Educational Testing Service, 1988).

25.   Linda Darling-Hammond, "Performance Based Assessment and Educational Equity," *Harvard Educational Review* 64:1 (1988).

26.   *Years of Promise*, xvii.

27.   *Ibid.*, 79.

28.   *Individuals with Disabilities Education Act*, P.L 101-476 (1990).

29.   J. Nisbet, *Education Reform: Summary and Recommendations: The National Reform Agenda and People with Mental Retardation: Putting People First* (Washington, DC: U.S. Department of Health and Human Services, 1994).

30.   D. Staub and C.A. Peck, "What Are the Outcomes for Nondisabled Students," *Educational Leadership* 52:4 (1994): 36–40.

Index

About Teaching Strategies, Inc.

Founded in 1988 by Diane Trister Dodge, Teaching Strategies, Inc. believes that the future of our country depends on our ability to nurture the optimal growth and development of every child. New research about the development of the brain underscores the vital importance of the first eight years of life. High quality early childhood programs develop strong partnerships with families to build the foundation children need to become enthusiastic life-long learners who succeed in school and in life. Teaching Strategies produces practical, developmentally appropriate curriculum and training materials and offers training programs and staff development services for teachers and parents. We publish more than 30 books and videos and train thousands of teachers each year.

About the Authors

Toni Bickart has taught the primary grades at The Sidwell Friends School in Washington, D.C., and is a Senior Associate and Director of Primary Grade Programs for Teaching Strategies, Inc. She has worked extensively as a teacher mentor in the D.C. Public Schools and presents workshops for teachers and parents around the country. In addition to her educational background, Ms. Bickart holds a Masters degree in Social Work from Columbia University. She is the parent of two children.

Diane Trister Dodge is President of Teaching Strategies, Inc. and the author of more than 20 books on early childhood education, including *The Creative Curriculum® for Early Childhood*, the country's second most used preschool/kindergarten model, and *A Parent's Guide to Early Childhood Education*, which has sold more than 500,000 copies. She holds a Masters degree in Early Childhood Education from the Bank Street College of Education and began her career first as a kindergarten teacher and then as the education coordinator for a Head Start program in rural Mississippi. Ms. Dodge is a well-known speaker and trainer and a former member of the Governing Board of the National Association for the Education of Young Children (NAEYC). She is the parent of three children.

Judy Jablon is an experienced classroom teacher, author, and staff development specialist. She spent twelve years in the classroom teaching grades one through four and holds a Masters degree in Early Childhood Education from the Bank Street College of Education. Ms. Jablon is a nationally-recognized expert on early childhood assessment. She is currently working on major school reform projects with the South Carolina Department of Education and the Maryland Department of Education.

Toni Bickart, Diane Trister Dodge, and Judy Jablon have nearly 70 years combined experience in education—as classroom teachers, curriculum developers, authors, teacher mentors, researchers, and staff developers. They previously collaborated on *Constructing Curriculum for the Primary Grades*, a resource for teachers that demonstrates how good instructional practices make curriculum meaningful for the children they teach. *Constructing Curriculum* has been used in schools across the country by thousands of teachers who want to create exciting classrooms of active learners.

Notes

A Note from Teaching Strategies, Inc.

Do you want to hear more? Teaching Strategies has a national network of experienced educators who work with principals, teachers, and parents to bring about the types of classrooms advocated in this book. The authors and these expert facilitators are available as speakers and workshop leaders for PTA/PTOs and teacher continuing education programs.

We would love to hear from you about your child's experiences in school and any suggestions you may have about parent involvement in education.

You can contact us at:

Teaching Strategies, Inc.
P.O. Box 42243
Washington, DC 20015
(800) 637-3652
Email: TSI7543@aol.com